Prayers For

God's

People

**THOMAS P.
ROBERTS**

WORSHIP
RESOURCES
FOR THE
CHRISTIAN YEAR

C.S.S. Publishing Co., Inc.
Lima, Ohio

Library of Congress Cataloging-in-Publication Data

Roberts, Thomas P., 1951-
  Prayers for God's people.

  1. Prayers. I. Title.
BV250.R59   264'.13   87-30154
ISBN 1-55673-025-X

8810 / ISBN 1-55673-025-X   PRINTED IN U.S.A.

To Mary

TABLE OF CONTENTS

Introduction

1 The Call to Worship *9*

2 Invocations and Opening Prayers *26*

3 Unison Prayers and Prayers of Confession *35*

4 Affirmations of Faith *55*

5 Pastoral Prayers and Prayers of Intercession *60*

6 Offertory Prayers *92*

7 Benedictions *100*

8 Special Services

Communion *110*

Christmas Eve *116*

Maundy Thursday *120*

Good Friday *126*

9 Topical Prayers and Prayers for Special
Occasions *130*

Introduction

This book was written out of my own need, as a pastor, for more worship resources, and I have already used all of the contents of this book in my worship services.

My own preference for worship language and imagery could be described as follows: I like the traditional, as long as it is not archaic; and I like the contemporary, as long as it is not faddish. Accordingly, I have used some of the traditional language for God ("Heavenly Father," "Lord," "King," etc.), though not exclusively. The debate continues as to how we should refer to God, and this is an issue which I regard with utmost seriousness. Nevertheless, in writing this book, I have drawn from my own faith experience and the language and imagery which accompany it. I would only hope that other ministers and worship leaders whose views differ from mine will accept the sincerity of this approach, and will make editorial (and theological) changes as they see fit.

Many of the other current books of worship resources are structured according to lectionary readings. There are advantages to that kind of format, but the format I have chosen should be equally useful in its own way. Even for the minister who uses the lectionary every week, it is not necessary to organize an entire worship service around a single theme or group of biblical passages.

It is generally agreed that the church is not obligated to observe every secular holiday and occasion that comes along, but I find that a single, topical prayer during the worship service (for Mother's Day, Memorial Day, Fourth of July, etc.), followed by a hymn response, will fulfill the needs of many worshipers, and will spare the minister from a lot of unnecessary criticism! Such topical prayers are found in Chapter Nine.

I have identified Scripture passages which were used in writing these worship resources. In some instances, a biblical phrase or idea is recaptured in a particular prayer or liturgy, and in other instances, the biblical references were used only as a starting point in the creative process. Unless otherwise indicated, the *Jerusalem Bible* translation (including the Apocrypha) was used. The only exception to this is for the Psalms, where the preferred translation was by the *Grail* (Published 1963, by Collins in Fontana Books, London). The numbering of the Psalms is according to the *Hebrew Bible*.

This book is dedicated to a very special person, the Rev. Mary Roberts, who is my wife; and I also want to express my deep affection for my parents, James and Sarah Roberts; my children, Marilyn and Kolby; and a loving, supportive congregation, with whom I have prayed all the *Prayers for God's People*.

Thomas P. Roberts
First United Methodist Church
Granada Hills, California

1

1. *Leader:* By day the Lord commands his steadfast love,
   People: **And at night his song is with me.**
   Leader: I will sing of his praise!
   People: **I will sing with joy!**
   Leader: For this is my God,
   People: **And I extol him, Lord and King.**

   Psalm 42:8, Exodus 15:1-6

2. *Leader:* Sun and moon! Bless the Lord.
   People: **Stars of heaven! Bless the Lord.**
   Leader: Showers and dew! Bless the Lord.
   People: **Clouds and wind! Bless the Lord.**
   Leader: Let all the earth bless our Creator.
   People: **For he has made all things and called them good.**

   Daniel 3:62-67

3. *Leader:* Sing a new song to the Lord!
   People: **Let the heavens rejoice and the earth be glad.**
   Leader: Sing to the Lord, and bless his name.
   People: **We will tell of God's wonders among all the peoples.**
   Leader: Honor and majesty go before him,
   People: **And strength and beauty are in his sanctuary.**

   Psalm 96:1-6 (RSV)

4. *Leader:* I will bless the Lord, who gives me counsel.
   People: **I say to the Lord, "You are my God."**
   Leader: I will keep the Lord ever in my sight.

People: **Because he is at my right hand, I shall stand firm.**
Leader: And so my heart rejoices and my soul is glad,
People: **For I know the fulness of joy in his presence.**

Psalm 16:1-9

5. *Leader:* Let us hear what the Lord God has to say.
   People: **He will speak peace to his people; to those who turn their hearts toward him.**
   Leader: Love and loyalty will meet.
   People: **Justice and peace will embrace.**
   Leader: Faithfulness will spring up from the earth,
   People: **And righteousness will look down from heaven.**

Psalm 85:8-11

6. *Leader:* I rejoiced when I heard them say,
   People: **"Let us go to God's house."**
   Leader: Surely the word of the Lord is to be trusted,
   People: **And holiness belongs to his house.**
   Leader: Sing to the Lord with thankfulness and joy.
   People: **Let all the people hear us and be glad.**

Psalm 122:1, Psalm 93:5

7. *Leader:* Let us give thanks to the Lord for his faithful love,
   People: **Which exceeds all that we have ever known.**
   Leader: Let us bless his name in the company of angels.
   People: **We will worship him in his holy sanctuary.**
   Leader: God answers our call in times of need,
   People: **And stretches out his hand to save us.**
   Leader: Let all the earth say of his kingdom,
   People: **"How great is the glory of the Lord!"**

Psalm 138

8. *Leader:* We come before God in the holiness of this
   sanctuary,
   People: **To gaze upon his strength and glory.**
   Leader: God has been our help through all the ages,
   People: **And within the shadow of his wings, he will keep
   us safe.**
   Leader: Surely the love of God is our greatest blessing,
   People: **And we will return our praise forever more.**

                                                          Psalm 63

9. *Leader:* It is good to give thanks to God;
   People: **To make music to his name;**
   Leader: To proclaim his love in the morning,
   People: **And his truth in the watches of night.**
   Leader: How great are all thy works.
   People: **Glory be to God! Amen!**

                                                    Psalm 92:1-3 (RSV)

10. *Leader:* From the heavens the Lord looks forth,
    People: **And sees the people of his kingdom.**
    Leader: He shapes the hearts of all who love him,
    People: **And makes his power and greatness known.**
    Leader: Consider all that God has done for you.
    People: **As for me, I will sing his praise.**

                                                Psalm 33:13-15, Tobit 13:2-8

11. *Leader:* Let us give thanks to God for his faithfulness and
    love,
    People: **Which exceed all our understanding.**
    Leader: For the Lord is on high, yet he looks on the lowly.
    People: **He is close to the broken-hearted.**
    Leader: God hears the words of our lips and knows the

meditations of our hearts.
People: **He increases the strength of our souls.**
Leader: Happy are those who trust in the Lord.
People: **We are the people he has called his own.**

Psalm 34:17-18, Psalm 33:12

12. *Leader:* Proclaim to the nations, "God is King."
People: **He established the world and it shall not be moved.**
Leader: Let the heavens rejoice and the earth be glad.
People: **Let the trees of the woods shout for joy.**
Leader: For the Lord is great and greatly to be praised,
People: **And he will reign over us by his mercy and righteousness.**

Psalm 96:10-13

13. *Leader:* Let us praise God's name with a song!
People: **We will glorify him with thanksgiving.**
Leader: Let us sing of his strength and steadfast love,
People: **For the Lord has been our stronghold in times of distress.**
Leader: Turn your hearts to the Lord,
People: **And he will show us the way.**

Psalm 59:16

14. *Leader:* My soul proclaims the greatness of the Lord,
People: **And my spirit rejoices in God my Savior.**
Leader: The Almighty has done great things for me,
People: **And holy is his name.**
Leader: His mercy is from age to age,
People: **And his faithfulness endures forever!**

Luke 1:46-55

15. *Leader:* Sing with joy to the Creator of the earth,
    People: **And proclaim the glory of his name.**
    Leader: Come and see what God has done.
    People: **How tremendous are all his deeds!**
    Leader: Then let our happiness be found in him,
    People: **For he rules with goodness by his might.**

Psalm 66:1-7 (RSV)

16. *Leader:* My heart is ready, O God; my heart is ready.
    People: **I will sing; I will sing of your praise.**
    Leader: I will worship you in the midst of your sanctuary.
    People: **I will proclaim your word among all the peoples.**
    Leader: Great is your love, and greatly to be praised.
    People: **For our praise is fitting from loyal hearts.**

Psalm 57:7-8, Psalm 48:1 (RSV), Psalm 33:1

17. *Leader:* Sing to the Lord! Make music to his name!
    People: **We will rejoice in the Lord and exult in his presence.**
    Leader: For God is in his holy dwelling,
    People: **And he gives a home to all who seek him.**
    Leader: Blessed are those who come in the name of the Lord;
    People: **For they receive blessings of power and strength in this place of worship.**

Psalm 68:3-6,35 Psalm 118:26

18. *Leader:* This I know, that God is on my side.
    People: **In God, whose word I love; in God, I trust and have no fear.**
    Leader: To him, I will offer my praise,
    People: **That I may walk before him in the light of life.**

Leader: O God, arise above the heavens! Let your glory
shine upon the earth!
People: **For your love reaches to the highest heavens and
your truth to the skies.**

Psalm 56:9 11, Psalm 56:13 (RSV), Psalm 57:11

19. *Leader:* O give thanks to the Lord our God,
People: **Who will keep his covenant with us.**
Leader: Sing unto the Lord, sing praises!
People: **And remember the wonderful works he has done.**
Leader: Let the hearts that seek the Lord rejoice in him,
People: **And give glory and honor to his holy name.**

Psalm 105:1-5

20. *Leader:* Let us worship the Lord, who is good and for-
giving,
People: **Who is full of love toward all who call upon him.**
Leader: Let us lift up our hearts and voices unto God,
People: **And seek his truth and mercy.**
Leader: Let all peoples and nations sing with joy
People: **To him, who alone is God.**

Psalm 86:5-10

21. *Leader:* Praise God in this holy place.
People: **Praise him in his mighty heavens!**
Leader: Praise God for his powerful deeds,
People: **And praise his exceeding greatness!**
Leader: God formed the depths of the earth,
People: **And the heights of the mountains are his.**
Leader: To him belongs the sea,
People: **And the dry land shaped by his hands.**
Leader: Come, let us worship the Lord.

People: **Let everything that lives and breathes give praise to the Lord!**

Psalm 150:1-2, Psalm 95:4-7

22. *Leader:* Who is like the Lord our God?
    People: **His glory and majesty cannot be compared.**
    Leader: Who has risen on high to his throne?
    People: **God lifts up the lowly and humble in heart.**
    Leader: Then let us look to the Lord and be radiant!
    People: **We will rejoice in him and give thanks for his mighty works!**

Psalm 113:5-7, Psalm 34:5

23. *Leader:* The earth is the Lord's and the fulness thereof,
    People: **The world and all its peoples.**
    Leader: Yours, O God, is the majesty and the power,
    People: **And the splendor, the triumph, and the glory.**
    Leader: From your hand come strength and power.
    People: **From your hand come greatness and might.**
    Leader: Blessed are you, O God, for ages unending;
    People: **For yours is the Kingdom forever!**

Psalm 24:1 (RSV), 1 Chronicles 29:10-12

24. *Leader:* The Lord is King!
    People: **Let the earth rejoice!**
    Leader: High above the nations is our God;
    People: **Above the heavens is his glory.**
    Leader: Then let our happiness be found in him,
    People: **And our hope in his love.**

Psalm 97:1, Psalm 113:4, Psalm 33:21-22

25. *Leader:* Mighty is our God and great is his power.
    People: **His wisdom is without measure.**
    Leader: He fixes the number of stars,
    People: **And calls each one by name.**
    Leader: Sing praise unto God, sing praise!
    People: **For God is the creator of all the earth.**
    Leader: Sing praise unto our Lord, sing praise!
    People: **Let the faithful rejoice in his glory.**

                                         Psalm 147: 4-5, Psalm 47:6-9

26. *Leader:* How lovely is your dwelling place,
    People: **O Lord, our God and King!**
    Leader: Happy are those who dwell within this house,
    People: **And forever sing of your praise.**
    Leader: Let our heart and soul ring out with joy,
    People: **To our God, the living God!**

                                         Psalm 84:1-5

27. *Leader:* Come, let us go to the place of the Lord,
    People: **That he may teach us of his ways.**
    Leader: Let us follow in the light of the Lord,
    People: **That we may walk in his paths.**
    Leader: Happy are those who acclaim such a king,
    People: **And find their joy each day in him.**

                                         Isaiah 2:3, Psalm 89:15-16

28. *Leader:* Consider the Lord and all his strength.
    People: **We remember his miracles and the command-
    ments he has spoken.**
    Leader: God has kept his covenant with us,
    People: **The promise he made for a thousand generations.**
    Leader: Surely goodness and mercy will follow us all the

days of our lives,

People: **And we will dwell forever in the house of the Lord!**

Psalm 105:4-8, Psalm 23:6

29. *Leader:* Let us bless the Lord at all times.
    People: **His praise will be ever on our lips.**
    Leader: The Lord has shown his love by the work of his hands;
    People: **And all his ways are faithful and just.**
    Leader: The righteousness of God is forever and ever,
    People: **And his kingdom endures from age to age.**

Psalm 34:1-2, Psalm 111:7-8

30. *Leader:* Sing a new song to the Lord,
    People: **For he has worked wonders.**
    Leader: He has made known his salvation,
    People: **And has shown justice to the nations.**
    Leader: Let the ocean waves thunder,
    People: **And the rivers clap their hands.**
    Leader: Let the hills ring out with joy,
    People: **For the Lord our God rules over the earth!**

Psalm 98:1-2, 7-9

31. *Leader:* Come, sing out your joy to the Lord.
    People: **For the Lord is our strength, our song, and our salvation.**
    Leader: Praise be to the One who saves us.
    People: **The Lord is our rock, our fortress, and our Savior.**
    Leader: Let us show our love unto God, in whom we take refuge.

People: **For the Lord is our shield, our help, and our
stronghold.**
Leader: A mighty God is our Lord!
People: **And we are the people of his kingdom!**

Psalm 18:1-2

32. *Leader:* Our help is in the name of the Lord,
People: **Who made heaven and earth.**
Leader: He is our Creator,
People: **And we belong to him.**
Leader: Blessed are those who hope in the Lord,
People: **For he bears our burdens and heals the broken-
hearted.**
Leader: He reveals to us deep and mysterious things,
People: **And the light of life dwells within him!**

Psalm 124:8, Psalm 100:3, Psalm 68:19-20, Daniel 2:22

33. *(For World Communion Sunday)*

Leader: God has called us into one and the same hope.
People: **There is one hope, one faith, one Lord.**
Leader: Grace has been given to us through Jesus Christ.
People: **There is one hope, one faith, one Lord.**
Leader: The unity of the Holy Spirit is the peace which
binds us together.
People: **There is one hope, one faith, one Lord.**
Leader: Let us preserve the unity of the Spirit through
our self-giving love.
People: **We do so according to the one God who is over
all and within all through Jesus Christ. Amen!**

Ephesians 4:1-6

34. *(For Advent)*

Leader: A voice cries in the wilderness:
People: **"Prepare the way of the Lord."**
Leader: Make a clear path for our God.
People: **Let every valley be filled in, and every mountain and hill be made low.**
Leader: Winding ways will be straightened,
People: **And rough roads made smooth.**
Leader: Then the glory of the Lord shall be revealed,
People: **And all his people shall see it and give thanks.**

Luke 3:1-6, Isaiah 40:1-11

35. *(For Advent)*

Leader: God has raised up for us a mighty Savior,
People: **Who has fulfilled the promises spoken by prophets.**
Leader: God has sent his Son to free us from our fears,
People: **And to guide us in the ways of peace.**
Leader: To us has been given the hope of salvation,
People: **By the tender mercy of God.**
Leader: Blessed be the Lord our God!
People: **For he has visited his people!**

Luke 1:67-79 (RSV)

36. *(For Advent)*

Leader: The Lord will come to save his people.
People: **Blessed are those who are ready to receive him.**
Leader: Let the wilderness and the dry lands exult!
People: **Let the deserts rejoice and bloom!**
Leader: Send victory like a dew, O heavens from above,

People: And let the earth open up to bring forth our
Savior.

Isaiah 35:1, 45:8

37. *(For Advent)*

Leader: The heavens proclaim the glory of God,
People: **And the skies show forth the work of his hands.**
Leader: Day to day brings forth the story,
People: **And night unto night makes known the message.**
Leader: Who is the King of Glory?
People: **The Lord, strong and mighty: he is the King of
Glory!**

Psalm 19:1-4, Psalm 24:8-10 (RSV)

38. *(For Advent)*

Leader: In many and various ways, God has spoken
through his prophets of old;
People: **But in our time, God speaks to us through his
Son.**
Leader: The Word was made flesh,
People: **And lives among us!**
Leader: Glory be to God!
People: **Glory to God in the highest!**

Hebrews 1:1-2, John 1:14

39. *(For Advent)*

Leader: Behold, the Prince of Peace is coming into the
world.
People: **He will free us from the yoke of our bondage.**

Leader: He will wield authority over the nations;
People: **And they will hammer their swords into plowshares, and their spears into sickles.**
Leader: Nation will not lift up sword against nation;
People: **Neither shall they learn war anymore.**

Isaiah 2:4

40. *(For Advent)*

Leader: How beautiful upon the mountains are the feet of him who brings good tidings;
People: **Who heralds peace and proclaims salvation.**
Leader: Let the Lord enter here.
People: **For the Lord, our God, is the King of Glory!**

Isaiah 52:7-10 (RSV)

41. *(For Christmas)*

Leader: Today a child is born,
People: **Who is Savior of the world.**
Leader: The Spirit of God shall rest upon him;
People: **The spirit of wisdom and understanding;**
Leader: The spirit of counsel and might;
People: **The spirit of knowledge and the fear of the Lord.**
Leader: On this day, a new light shines upon the earth.
People: **For Christ is born unto us. Amen!**

Isaiah 11:2

42. *(For Epiphany)*

Leader: A hallowed day has dawned upon us,
People: **For today a great light has shone upon the earth.**

Leader: Behold, the Lord has come with power,
People: To enlighten the eyes of his people.
Leader: The Lord is our King and Savior.
People: Great is his beginning, and his reign will have no end.

43. *(For Epiphany)*

Leader: O God, send forth your light and truth.
People: Let these be my guide.
Leader: Let me come to the place where you dwell,
People: For you are the God of my life.
Leader: Then I will sing forever of your love,
People: And I will rejoice in your glory.

Psalm 43:3-4, Psalm 89:1-2

44. *(For Lent)*

Leader: Though I have fallen,
People: Yet I shall rise.
Leader: When I dwell in the darkness,
People: The Lord will be my light.
Leader: As for my part, I will look to the Lord.
People: I will rejoice to see the rightness of his ways.
Leader: My hope is in the God of my salvation.
People: My God will hear me.

Micah 7:7-9

45. *(For Lent)*

Leader: Open to me the gates of holiness.
People: I will enter and give thanks.

Leader: This is the Lord's own gate,
People: **Where the faithful shall enter.**
Leader: Blessed are those who come in the name of the Lord,
People: **For they will find peace and joy within the house of God.**

Psalm 118:19-20, 26

46. *(For Lent)*

Leader: Come, glorify the Lord with me.
People: **Together we will praise his name.**
Leader: Seek the Lord, and he will answer us.
People: **God will set us free from our fears.**
Leader: See that the Lord is good!
People: **For his steadfast love endures forever!**

Psalm 34:3-8

47. *(For Lent)*

Leader: We come to the house of the Lord,
People: **Where we enter and give thanks.**
Leader: God hears us in our prayers,
People: **And has given us victory in Christ.**
Leader: The stone which the builders rejected
People: **Has become for us a cornerstone.**
Leader: This is the Lord's own doing,
People: **And it is a wonder to our eyes.**

Psalm 118:19-24

48. *(For Palm Sunday)*

Leader: Rejoice with heart and soul.
People: **We will shout with gladness!**
Leader: See now, your king comes to you.
People: **He comes triumphant and victorious, but humble and riding upon a colt.**
Leader: He will proclaim peace among the nations,
People: **And his dominion shall extend to the ends of the earth.**
Leader: Blessed is he who comes in the name of the Lord.
People: **Hosanna in the highest heavens!**

Zechariah 9:9-10, Luke 19:38

49. *(For Easter)*

Leader: Lo, I tell you a mystery. We shall not all sleep, but we shall all be changed,
People: **In a moment, in the twinkling of an eye, at the last trumpet sound.**
Leader: For the trumpet will sound, and the dead will be raised imperishable, and we shall all be changed.
People: **For this perishable nature must put on the imperishable, and this mortal nature must put on immortality.**
Leader: Then shall come to pass the saying that is written: Death is swallowed up in victory.
People: **O Death, where is thy victory? O Death, where is thy sting?**
Leader: Thanks be to God, who gives us the victory through Jesus Christ our Lord.
People: **Amen**

1 Corinthians 15:51-58

50. *(For Easter)*

Leader: Send victory like a rain from heaven.
People: **Let the clouds pour it down,**
Leader: Let the earth open up,
People: **That salvation may spring forth.**
Leader: Let righteousness blossom at its side,
People: **For God has made it that way.**
Leader: Let every knee bend down and every tongue confess, saying:
People: **Jesus Christ is Lord!**
Leader: The Lord is risen.
People: **He is risen indeed!**

Isaiah 45:8-26

51. *(For Eastertide)*

Leader: The night is over, and the light is shining.
People: **Let us walk in the light, for Christ is the light.**
Leader: God's truth and grace will be with him,
People: **And his name shall be exalted above all others.**
Leader: Let us proclaim the risen Christ to the ends of the earth,
People: **That even generations to come may know of his glory!**

52. *(For Pentecost)*

Leader: It shall be as God declares,
People: **That he will pour out his Spirit among all people.**
Leader: The young will see new visions,
People: **And the old will dream dreams.**
Leader: God will renew the face of the earth,
People: **And the Holy Spirit will fill the hearts of the faithful.**

Joel 3:1-5

2

1.   O God of Light and Love: We thank you for bringing
us to this time together. As we feel the warmth of the
morning sun, refreshing and renewing us for another day,
we are reminded of how your love in Christ renews us for
the call to discipleship. Let us offer ourselves to you in
a spirit of worship and exaltation, for surely you dwell
in our midst. Amen

2.   Your words are Spirit, O God, and they are life. You
bring us a message of peace which stretches into eternity.
So comfort us by your presence, and guide us by your purpose, as we offer ourselves to you in worship. Amen

John 6:63

3.   We enter this place, O God, knowing that it shall be
to us a house of prayer. We come with the assurance that
you care for us and accept us as we are. Make your will
known to us this day by the unfolding of your word,
through Jesus Christ our Lord. Amen

Isaiah 56:6-7

4.   Eternal God, our Father: You have created the world
in wonder and mystery. Your Spirit moves us in worship,
as we give you thanks for the many blessings of life and
love. Let us listen for your word, and be empowered by
it, through Christ our Lord. Amen

5.   O Lord our God: As even the heavens cannot contain you, how much less would this sanctuary where we draw near. Yet you hear us in our prayers, and you watch over us both night and day. Surely your Spirit dwells within us. We call upon your name in worship, and we seek the promise of your peace, your mercy, and your grace. Amen

1 Kings 8:27-30

6.   God of grace and glory: We have gathered together in the awareness of your everlasting love. We thank you for the presence of your Spirit, which enables us to live with confidence and joy. As we lift up our words of prayer and our songs of praise, we give ourselves to you in a spirit of true worship. Amen

7.   O God of truth and Lord of life: You have called us to this time and place to be a worshiping people. Let us be transformed by your love and become faithful witnesses to your saving grace. For to you, O Lord, is the greatness, the power, the glory, the victory, and the majesty; for all that is in the heavens and on earth is thine alone. Amen

1 Chronicles 29:11 (RSV)

8.   Almighty God: As we gather in this time of worship, let us share in the power of your Holy Spirit. And by this power, fill our faith with goodness; our goodness with knowledge; our knowledge with godliness; our godliness with kindness; and our kindness with love. Amen

2 Peter 1:4-7

9.   Lift up the light of your face upon us, O God, and

make us a light unto the world. In our worship and through
the service of our love, let our light so shine before others
that they may see our good works, and give glory to your
name. Amen

Matthew 5:14-16

10.   You are Spirit, O God, and those who worship you
must worship in spirit and in truth. Open our hearts to
receive the promises of your word, and grant that we may
surrender our will unto yours. For not to us, but to your
name belong all glory and honor. Help us to share in these
blessings as we gather now in our worship. Amen

John 4:24

11.   O God, the fountain of life and light: We who enter
this place of worship find our happiness in you. Let the
words of our prayers flow out of what fills our hearts,
for we are grateful for the magnitude of your love, which
surpasses all that we could ask or think. Let there be rejoicing and gladness among all the people who seek you
and call upon the name of Jesus Christ, our Lord. Amen

Luke 6:45

12.   Speak to us, O God, through our silence; speak to us
as we offer our prayers, our gifts, and our worship; speak
to us through the proclamation of your Word and in every dimension of your power, that we may be still and
know that you are God. Amen

13.   Dear Heavenly Father, we come to this sanctuary in
quietness and reverence, for surely you are in this place.

Let your Spirit rest upon us, and we shall live with confidence and hope. Show us the wonders of your redeeming love and the joy of serving you. Amen

14.   Eternal God: Help us to use our faith as a foundation, and build our lives upon it, always praying in the Holy Spirit. Reassure us in our doubts; rescue us from the perils of life; and free our minds from all our burdens, so that we may set our hope on nothing less than the grace given us in Christ Jesus. Amen

Jude 1:20-23

15.   Almighty God, the source of all good things: We enter this sanctuary to draw upon your strength and wisdom. You uphold our lives; you hear our prayers; you know our needs before we even ask you. We will praise your name, and open our hearts to receive your many blessings through Christ our Lord. Amen

16.   O God of all the ages: As we join together in worship, we realize that we are part of an entire community of faith. Let your will be our heritage forever, and your love be a source of everlasting joy. Help us to proclaim your word among all your peoples, as we also keep it close to our own hearts. Amen

17.   Eternal Spirit of God: We who gather here today are part of the household of faith that has prophets and apostles for its foundation, and Jesus Christ as its cornerstone. Through our worship, let us grow together into one holy temple of the Lord. For so long as your Spirit dwells within us, surely we will dwell with you. Amen

Ephesians 2:19-22

18.   O God who is good and forgiving, and abounding in
steadfast love: We lift up our souls unto you. In times of
need, we seek your help, knowing that you hear our prayers
and preserve our lives according to your faithfulness. There
is no power in heaven or on earth like you, O God, for
you alone have done wondrous deeds. And so we offer
our praise with a fulness of heart, and by our worship,
we will glorify your name forever. Amen

Psalm 86:4-10

19.   O God of truth and light: Help us to enter your house
of worship with a sincerity of heart and a spirit of hope.
Keep us firm in the faith we profess, for surely Christ is
in our midst. Let us be concerned for one another as we
join together in fellowship, and let us respond to the needs
we see in others through our prayers and our works of
love. We ask in Christ's name, Amen.

Hebrews 10:22-25

20.   Your will, O God, stands firm forever and your truth
endures from age to age, like the earth you have created.
Let your face shine upon us this day, and fill us with your
life-giving Spirit, that we may rejoice and return praise
unto you. Amen

Psalm 119:88-91, 175

21.   Lord, you have been our dwelling place through all
generations of time. Even before the mountains were
brought forth or the earth took form, you were God, from
everlasting to everlasting. We are glad for our lives, and
we ask that you make us aware of your constant and abiding love, through Jesus, our Christ. Amen

Psalm 90:1-2 (RSV)

22.   Almighty and everlasting God: Send your grace upon this church and all who enter its doors, that this may be a place where brokenness finds healing, and loneliness finds belonging, and emptiness finds meaning. Remind us of our identity as a people of faith, as we call upon your name and seek your goodness and mercy through all of our days. Amen

23.   O Lord God, our Shepherd: Bring your people to pasture, the flock that is your heritage. We entrust ourselves to you. We seek to follow wherever you would lead us. For you have shown us faithfulness and mercy. Let us now show you our love. Amen

Micah 7:14-20

24.   Almighty and gracious God: We rejoice by dwelling in your sanctuary, for all of us have found a home in you. We trust in your rule over our world and within our own lives, because you are the Creator and Preserver of all things. So let us praise you for your goodness and abide by your commandments, for to you belong all power and glory, forever and ever. Amen

25. *(For Advent)*

    O God of Eternal Light: We come today seeking you in some special way. Yet we are reminded that you first sought us through your Son, the Christ. So let us rejoice in the light of your word made flesh, and praise the glory of his name, Jesus Christ our Lord. Amen

26. *(For Advent)*

O God of Everlasting Love: As the spirit of Christmas is felt in so many places of our world, let the spirit of Christ dwell within our hearts so that we may truly belong to him. We rejoice in the message of his birth, which brings with it a great comfort and a sure hope.

Let this time of worship and celebration be a time to renew our faith and empower us for discipleship, through Christ our Lord. Amen

27. *(For Advent)*

Almighty God: You have brought us again to this joyous season when we celebrate the birth of your Son. We pray that his spirit will be born anew in our hearts today. May the peace of Christ be our comfort and guide, as we praise his name above all others; that at the name of Jesus, every knee should bow in heaven and on earth, and every tongue confess that Jesus Christ is Lord. Amen

Philippians 2:10-11 (RSV)

28. *(For Christmas Eve)*

Eternal God our Father: We have come together this evening to share in the special joy of Christmas. We give thanks for family and friends who have drawn near to us in this hour. Let us lift up our voices to proclaim your mighty deed to the world, and to confess that you are God and we are your people. In the spirit of your Son, the Christ, let the church say together, Amen.

29. *(For Christmas)*

Dear Heavenly Father: We come seeking the Christ so that we may follow him all of our days. And whenever the manger in Bethlehem seems far removed from our world, the miracle breaks in upon our lives again.

For to us a child is born. To us a Son is given, and the glory of his grace has been revealed. We rejoice in his coming, and we receive his word with grateful hearts. Amen

Isaiah 9:6

30. *(For Lent)*

Almighty God, our source of strength and salvation: We come to this place of worship to ask for the forgiveness of our sins; to be comforted by your grace; to be uplifted by the word proclaimed; and to be guided toward that life which reflects the truth of your Gospel. We ask these things in the spirit of Christ. Amen

31. *(For Lent)*

Remember us in your mercy, O God, according to the love you have shown throughout all the generations. You are the rock, the stronghold, and the foundation upon which we stand. Help us to observe your commandments, and keep them close to our hearts; for those who put their trust in you will not be disappointed. Amen

Psalm 25:4-9, Psalm 62:1-2

32. *(For Lent)*

We who gather here call upon your name, O God. Let the contrite heart and the humble spirit be acceptable unto you. Grant us deliverance from our sins, and make us worthy of your many blessings.

By the light given us in your Son, the Christ, help us to walk in the paths that he walks, and be guided by his truth. We ask in his name, Amen.

Daniel 3:39-43

33. *(For Easter)*

God of Grace and God of Glory: On this joyous day, we come together to praise you for your mighty works.

As we feel the freshness of nature around us, let us also feel your renewing forces within our world, bringing new life out of death, hope out of despair, and victory out of destruction. For all these things have been revealed to us through the resurrection of your Son.

Let the spirit of the risen Christ dwell within our hearts and fill us with love, so that we may follow him all of our days. Amen

3

1. *Leader:* Remember how Jesus said, "I have come not to condemn the world, but to save it." In confidence and hope, let us pray to almighty God.

People: O God of steadfast love: We cannot discern all our errors, or know all the flaws that lie hidden within us. But you know us as we are, and you have restored our souls by your mercy and grace. Help us to trust in your rule over us so that we will find the true source of joy to our hearts. Instill in us your heavenly commandments, that they may bring justice to our world and fill our own lives with your holiness. Amen

Leader: Hear the good news: The new creation is here. For the old has passed away and the new has come. In Christ, we are a new creation.

John 12:47, Psalm 19, 2 Corinthians 5:14-17

2. We thank you, O God, for the gift of faith, which promises us the blessings we hope for, and confirms for us the invisible powers of heaven. Through faith, we know that the world was created by your Word, and that you are the source of every living thing.

We are grateful for the enduring witness of your people of faith, who have rejoiced in the blessings they received from you and have looked forward to their destiny within your kingdom.

Let us profit by their example as we draw near to you in faith, and acknowledge your goodness toward all who call upon your name. Amen

Hebrews 11:1-40

3.   Eternal God: We thank you for the Christ, who by his righteousness, became the sacrifice that took away our sins and the sins of the world. He revealed to us the love and justice which come from you alone.

Help us now to keep the commandments of Christ, so that your truth will abide in us. For it is by our obedience to your Word that we will know you and that our love for you will be perfected. Let us walk in the ways that Jesus walked, and we will be sure of our union with you and with one another. We ask these things in his name. Amen

1 John 2:1-5

4.   O God who gives us life and breath: You have made us out of the goodness of creation. Instill in us a sense of responsible living, so that we may fulfill our human potential. Help us to care for our physical health, to control our desires, to free our minds from harmful thoughts, and to use our time and energy in constructive ways. Give us the vision to behold the beauty of nature and to live in harmony with it.

In all these ways, let us affirm our own worthiness and reveal the glory of your work. Amen

5.   O God of eternal light: Help us to be your faithful servants according to the example of Christ. Let us not strive merely for the approval of others, but to glorify your name. Free us from selfish passions that attack the soul, and save us from ambitions that cannot satisfy us. And as we pray to you, let us always ask for what we need, rather than what we want. For then we shall truly know the sustaining gifts of life; faith, hope, and love, as they flow from you. Amen

James 4:1-10

6.   God of Spirit and truth: Let us not call evil good, and good evil; or put darkness for light, and light for darkness. If we would have wisdom, let it be the wisdom of your ways and not our own. For you have called us to a life in the Spirit. Let us now walk by the Spirit in all that we do and in all that we are. Amen

Leader: Hear the good news: The Lord is in your midst. He will exult with joy over you and will renew you by his love.

Isaiah 5:20-21, 1 Peter 1:15-16, Zephaniah 3:14-18

7.   Most merciful and loving God: Let us not love merely by word or by speech, but in deed and in truth. And through this love, we can be certain that we belong to the truth.

If ever our conscience is troubled, if ever we bring condemnation upon ourselves, remind us that your power surpasses all things. Help us to walk with confidence, keeping your commandments, and living the kind of life you intended for us. Let your Spirit dwell within our hearts as it also dwells within the living Christ. We pray in his name, Amen.

Leader: Friends, hear the good news: The Lord will keep you from all evil; he will keep your life. The Lord will keep your going out and your coming in from this time forth and forever more.

1 John 3:18-24, Psalm 121:7-8 (RSV)

8.   Help us, O God, to put our trust in you. Let us not be swept away by evil, or misled by false promises. For

flight cannot rescue the swift; the strong will find their strength useless; and the mighty will be powerless to save. You alone are the source of salvation. Show us your mercy, and enable us to walk toward the paths of perfection, knowing that your love is ever before our eyes. Amen

Amos 2:14-15

9.   Eternal God: We thank you for your peace, which you give us through the Lord Jesus Christ. Through him, we have received the grace in which we live, and we have the hope of sharing in his glory.

If ever we should suffer, we ask that you give us patience, for we know that patience brings us perseverance, and perseverance brings us hope, and hope cannot disappoint us, because your love has been poured into our hearts through the Holy Spirit. Amen

Romans 5:1-5

10. *Leader:* Seek the Lord while he may be found. Call upon him while he is near.

People: Creator, Redeemer God: Bring light to our eyes and reveal to us whatever is hidden by darkness. Show us the secret intentions of our own hearts so that we will not be enslaved to sin. You have called us to a life of freedom in Christ. Let us now use our freedom to act with justice and speak with truth; to stand boldly in the world and live by faith. We ask these things in Jesus' name. Amen

Leader: The Lord is compassionate and merciful. As far

as east is from west, so far does he remove our
transgressions from us. Through Christ, we are
reconciled to God, and renewed in our power to
serve him and one another.

Isaiah 55:6 (RSV), Psalm 103:8, 12

11.   O God of Perfect love: If we are without love, then
we speak with an empty voice. If we give of our posses-
sions, but not in the spirit of love, then we have failed
to accomplish your will. We can probe the mysteries of
life, but without love, we will lack understanding.

Show us patience and kindness. Keep us from being
jealous or boastful, selfish or rude. Let us rejoice in the
good we see in others, rather than taking account of sin.
Make us ready to forgive, to trust, and to endure in all
things.

Help us to seek after the higher gifts of life: the gifts
of faith, hope, and love. We know that the love you have
for us, O God, will never end, and that the love we share
with you and with one another is the greatest gift of all.
Amen

1 Corinthians 13

12. *Leader:* Jesus calls us, as his disciples, to stand before God
and acknowledge our sin. Let us do so in the assurance of God's forgiving love.

People: Almighty God: We who have sown much, sometimes have harvested little. We may eat our fill,
but still be hungry. We have clothes to wear, but
do not always feel warm. We strive to have more,
even when we have enough.

Free us from our preoccupation with money
and material things. Let us not plan our lives according to what we can afford, but according to
the quality of life which you have shown us in
Christ. Help us to find an inner peace and contentment within ourselves by seeking the treasures of heaven, for there will our heart be also.
Amen

Leader: God is merciful and does not treat us according
to our faults. For as the heavens are high above
the earth, so great is his compassion for those who
love him.

People: Thanks be to God, and forget none of his
benefits. Amen

Haggai 1:1-8, Psalm 103:2, 8-11

13.   Dear God: Grant us your wisdom in all that we do;
for your wisdom is pure and makes for peace. It is kindly
and considerate, open to reason, and full of mercy. Your
wisdom is without uncertainty or insincerity, but shows
itself in kindness and virtue. We give thanks, O God, for
the harvest of your goodness, which has been sown in wisdom by those who love you. Amen

James 3:13-15 (RSV)

14.   God of truth and strength: Help us to lead a life worthy of our calling. Save us from needless strife and dissension, but fill us with indignation for the injustices of
our world. Do not shield us from the sufferings of hunger and disease, or the violence of war.
        We seek to serve you and one another in the unity of

your Spirit, knowing that all things work together
for good for those who love you. Amen

Leader: Friends, hear the good news: By the grace of our
Lord Jesus Christ, all things are brought together
in unity. All things are reconciled through him
and for him, everything in heaven and on earth.

Romans 8:28, Colossians 1:15-20

15. Leader: The Spirit comes to help us in our weakness, even
as we struggle to express ourselves in prayer. Let
us trust that God will understand everything within our hearts.

People: O God of mercy: Help us to be steadfast in our
own integrity, and undeterred by the power of
sin. In the face of all our limitations and through
all our struggles, let us remember to choose life
as it abundantly flows from your Spirit. For you
have taught us that whosoever lives in you shall
never die, according to the promises of Christ our
Lord. Amen

Leader: The Lord looks upon those who revere him, on
those who hope in his love. His own designs shall
stand forever, and the plans of his heart from age
to age. Amen

Romans 8:26, Ezekiel 18:25-28, Psalm 33:11, 18

16.   Eternal God: Show us the way of compassion, kindness, gentleness, and patience. Help us to bear with one
another and be forgiving, as you have forgiven us. Let
the peace of Christ dwell within our hearts and bring us
together as one body.

May your word, in all its richness, find a home in us, and so empower us to teach others of your wisdom. With gratitude, we give ourselves to you, O God, and ask that in all we do, by word and deed, we do in the name of our Lord Jesus Christ. Amen

Colossians 3:12-17

17. *Leader:* God will hear the confessions of our hearts and give us comfort. So let us open ourselves unto him.

People: Almighty and merciful God: Help us to stand firm when we face the trials of life. When cares increase in our hearts, bring consolation to our souls. Remind us that we are never tempted by anything but our own desires, and that we are capable of avoiding the ways of sin.

Help us to accept your word and submit to your will as your Spirit dwells within us. For you have brought us forth, O God, to be the children of your heavenly light. Let us seek after the good and perfect things which come from above, and bear the fruits of your righteousness. Amen

Leader: Hear the good news: The word of faith which we proclaim is very near to you; it is on your lips and in your heart. Everyone who calls upon the name of the Lord will be forgiven and justified, according to the grace given in Christ. Amen

James 1:12-27, Romans 10:8-13

18. *Leader:* When we offer ourselves to God, sin will no longer dominate our lives. Let us seek God's grace

as we make our prayers of confession.

People: O God of kindness and compassion: Keep me from the way of error, and teach me your ways. Do not take the word of truth from my lips, for I trust in your holy will. I know my offenses, and my sin is ever before me. Against you alone have I sinned. Have mercy upon me, most merciful God. Create a pure heart within me, and give me again the joy of your saving help. Amen

Leader: It is by God's own compassion that we are saved. We have been renewed by the power of the Holy Spirit, which God so generously poured out to us through our Savior Jesus Christ.

Psalm 51:3-10, Titus 3:4-7

19.   Spirit of the living God: Help us to keep this commandment of Christ — that we love one another as he has loved us. And let this love make demands upon us, so that we will love not only those who love us, but even our adversaries as well.

Just as your sun shines and your rain falls upon the whole of creation and all of its peoples, so may our love spread out to all the world. We ask in Jesus' name, Amen.

John 15:17, Matthew 5:43-48

20.   Almighty God, from whom all creatures receive life and breath: Help us to receive your word as a vital power within our lives. Fill our thoughts with everything that is true and noble, good and pure, everything that we love and honor, and everything that is virtuous and worthy of your praise. Enable us to do all the things which you call

us to do, for you have called even the greatest among us
to be your servants.

Whatever may be our hurts or needs, we still pray to
you in thanksgiving. And we ask that you sustain us in
our faith, that it may lead to even greater faith. May your
peace, which is beyond all our understanding, keep our
hearts and minds in the love and knowledge of your Son,
Jesus Christ our Lord. Amen

Philippians 4:6-9

21.   We thank you, O God, for the gift of salvation through
your Son, the Christ, and for the example of his life. He
ate with sinners; he spoke with tax collectors; he loved the
unlovable; he accepted the unacceptable. He brought healing and wholeness to all who sought his grace. Help us
to follow in his path, and share in his reconciling love with
one another. Amen

22. *Leader:* God searches our hearts and knows us. He shows
his great love for us, and saves us by his hand.
Let us come to God in prayer.

People: O God of all goodness and power: You have
taught us, in Christ, that no one can serve two
masters; for either we will hate the one and love
the other, or we will be devoted to the one and
despise the other. We cannot be both your servant and a slave to material things.

So let us not be anxious about our life, what we
shall eat or drink, or what we shall wear. Surely
life is more than food and the body more than
clothing.

Keep us from being consumed by our worries, and remind us that as you clothe the grass of the fields, so also will you provide for our needs. Help us to seek first your kingdom and righteousness, and trust that all other things will be added unto us as well. Amen

Leader: Whoever is born of God overcomes the world, and it is our faith which brings us this victory through Christ our Lord. Amen

Psalm 17:1-7, Matthew 6:24-34, 1 John 5:4

23.   Almighty and everlasting God: Help us to be content in our weaknesses. For when we are weak, we find the true source of our strength in Christ. Even though our bodies may fail us, we pray that the power of Christ will renew us in our inner spirit.

Surely his grace is sufficient for our every need, and our power through him will be made perfect in weakness. We pray these things in his name. Amen

2 Corinthians 12:1-10

24. *Leader:* Our hope is in the name of the Lord. Let us trust in him and pour out the confessions of our hearts.

People: Eternal God: We confess that sometimes we have been unwilling to pay the costs of what we truly value. Forgive us for seeking security without commitment, rewards without labor, happiness without sacrifice, and faith without discipline. Help us to bear the costs of all that we seek, especially the cost of our discipleship in Christ. By his example, let us live in the fulness of life and discover what it means to be genuinely human. In his name we pray. Amen

25. *Leader:* Remember that Christ experienced our human
weaknesses, and was tempted in every way that
we are, though he was without sin. Through him,
we shall have mercy as we make our confessions
before God.

People: O God of Spirit and truth: Save us from the bat-
tles we fight within ourselves — wanting things
we cannot own, having desires which we cannot
satisfy. In your generosity toward us, let us not
be envious of others. Preserve the health of our
souls, and save us from the personal ambitions
which bring disharmony among us.

Let us not be captivated by the wisdom of the
world; but let us aspire toward your wisdom,
which transcends the world and fills us with a
spirit of kindness and charity. Help us, O God,
to seek after your peace, which sows the seeds
of holiness within our own hearts and among all
those whom we love. Amen

Leader: Nothing can come between us and the love of
God. Even though we encounter the trials of life,
God's power will make us triumphant.

People: Amen! Thanks be to God!

Hebrews 4:14-16, James 3:16—4:3, Romans 8:35-39

26. *Leader:* God encourages all those whose hope is failing.
Let us turn away from our old selves, and return
to God in prayer.

People: To live is to risk, and yet we confess, O God, our
reluctance to do so. We want success without

experiencing failure, opportunity without taking initiative, and acceptance without making ourselves vulnerable. Open our hearts and minds to welcome new challenges and to receive new people into our lives. Strengthen our faith in you, and help us to be more giving of ourselves and more trusting in one another. Amen

Leader: God will keep you safe in his care, and by his faithfulness, he will protect and defend you.

People: Let us live unto the Lord! Amen!

Sirach 17:24-25

27. *Leader:* Whoever follows the Lord will have the light of life. Let us seek his help as we offer ourselves in prayer.

People: If you, O God, should account for our guilt, none of us would be found worthy. But there is mercy within you, and we gratefully receive your message of forgiveness. Keep us from evil, and bless us with the spiritual blessings of heaven. Choose us this day as the children of your kingdom, so that we may live through love in Christ, and praise the glory of your name. Amen

Leader: Hear the good news: God has saved us from the overpowering hand of sin. He will bring comfort to our hearts and will turn our sorrow into gladness.

Psalm 130, Colossians 1:3-6, Jeremiah 31:10-13

28. O God of all the ages: You chose what was foolish by

the world's standards in order to shame the wise, and you chose what was weak in order to shame the strong. Those whom the world found low and despised were the ones you called to do your work and to proclaim the message of your love and forgiveness.

As we answer our call to discipleship, let us not boast of our accomplishments, but only of our constant need for you. For you have given us Jesus Christ as our source of life, and in him we find our wisdom, our virtue, our holiness, and our freedom. Let us so follow him by the power of your Spirit. Amen

1 Corinthians 1:26-31

29. *Leader:* The Lord is good and forgiving, and full of love to all who call upon him. Let us now make our prayers of confession.

People: Creator God: You have taught us that what we sow we shall also reap. If we sow selfishness, we will reap loneliness; if we sow dishonesty, we will reap unhappiness; if we sow anger, we will reap dissension. Restore a spirit of gentleness within us. Let us not deceive ourselves by vain-glory, but find our happiness in you. May we never grow weary of our tasks, but always strive toward your good, which is rich with opportunity. We pray in the name of Christ, who is the source of eternal meaning to our lives. Amen

Leader: The will of God is not beyond our strength or reach. It is very near to us. Indeed, it is within us, so that we can follow it.

People: Thanks be to God for his saving help. Amen

Psalm 86:5, Galatians 6:7-10, Deuteronomy 30:10-14

30.   Almighty and everlasting God: Let us not honor you with our lips whenever our hearts are distant from you. We confess that sometimes we get caught up in details and neglect the weightier matters of justice, mercy, and faith. Keep us from being consumed by our own problems so that we will remember the needs of others and the concerns of our world.

Let your Spirit take root in our lives; let it blossom and grow, that we may find peace within ourselves and seek after all that is worthy in your name. Amen

Leader: Hear what the Lord proclaims: "I shall give you a new heart; a new spirit I will put within you. I will cause you to walk according to my ways so that you shall be my people and I will be your God."

Matthew 23:23-26, Ezekiel 36:23-28 (RSV)

31.   O God of compassion and understanding: Keep us from turning our self-worth into self-centeredness. We seek to live in the world with courage and confidence, and yet remain humble before you. We want to show personal resourcefulness, but also recognize our dependence upon you.

Help us to hold on to all that you have taught us, and rejoice in the good you have given us. Fill our hearts and minds with the love and knowledge of Jesus Christ our Lord, who by his suffering, took our faults upon himself that we might be restored to wholeness. Amen

Leader: God loves us with so much love that he is generous in his mercy. Though we were with sin, God
brought us to new life in Christ.

People: Amen!

Ephesians 2:1-10

32. *Leader:* Seek the Lord, all you who believe in his name,
and your hearts will be uplifted; for the Lord
listens to those who are in need. Let us pray:

People: Dear God and Father of all humankind: As you
call us to a life of liberty through Christ, help us
to resist the yoke of sin. Let us not abuse our freedom by resorting to self-indulgence, but make us
free to serve one another in works of love. We
accept your commandment to love our neighbors
as ourselves, and we strive to live by it. Help us
to carry out all our good intentions, and so build
up the community of your people, through Jesus Christ our Lord. Amen

Leader: Such is the richness of grace: That in Christ, we
gain our freedom by the forgiveness of sins, and
we are claimed as God's own.

People: How good is the Lord to all of us! Amen

Galatians 5:13-18, Ephesians 1:5-10

33. *(For Advent)*

God of grace and glory: As we enter this holy season
of Advent, we look again for the light of Christ to enter
our lives in a new and challenging way.

It is a light which shines upon our world and each one of us. It reveals the intentions of our hearts and the mysteries of creation. It gives direction to those who feel lost by their fears, their hurts, and their doubts.

You have promised us, O God, that the light will never desert us. For nothing in heaven or on earth can ever separate us from your great love in Christ. In his name, we pray. Amen

34. *(For Advent)*

Almighty and everlasting God: Let our hearts and minds be so open to receiving your word that even a little child may lead us. Show us the way to Bethlehem, that we too, may share in the joy of the Christ child and tell of his glory.

Surely our hope is renewed in the Christmas story, and we will find our fulfillment in the One who dwelt among us. Amen

35. *(For Advent)*

Eternal God: You have brought the light of Christ to shine out of darkness. It is a light upon all the earth, and it is full of majesty and wonder. Let it break in upon our lives again and again, enabling us to know his truth and be transformed by his power. We ask in Christ's name. Amen

36. *(For Lent)*

Leader: God is just in all his ways and loving in all his

deeds. He will hear the confessions of our hearts. Let us pray together:

People: Help us, O God, to overcome the power of sin. Let us never lose sight of our Lord Jesus Christ, who guides us in faith, and who for our sake, endured the cross, disregarding the shamefulness of it, and from now on has taken his place within your heavenly kingdom. As Christ endured the hostility of sinners, so may we endure the struggles that are before us, and not grow weary or fainthearted. We pray in his name. Amen

Leader: Jesus said, "Shoulder my yoke and learn from me, for I am gentle and humble in heart, and you will find rest for your souls. Yes, my yoke is easy and my burden light."

Psalm 145:17-19, Hebrews 12:1-4 (RSV), Matthew 11:28-30

37. *(For Lent)*

God of mercy and grace: We remember the example of Christ, who underwent temptation, and forsook the powers of the world in order to have the power of the Holy Spirit. He was obedient unto death, even death on the cross.

As we share in his sufferings, let us also share in his hope. And help us to offer unto others, in their sorrows, the comfort we have received from you. Amen

Leader: God loved the world so much that he gave his only Son, so that everyone who believes in him may not be lost, but will have eternal life.

2 Corinthians 1:1-7, John 3:16

38. *(For Lent)*

O God of eternal love: As a body dies when it is separated from the spirit, so will our faith die if it becomes separated from doing good deeds in your name. Help us to be true followers of Christ, to take up his cross, and to offer ourselves in service and in love for his sake. In so doing, let us not seek after worldly recognition, but a closer relationship with our Lord and Savior, Jesus Christ. We pray in his name. Amen

Mark 8:34

39. *(For Lent)*

Leader: Anyone who is joined to the Lord is of one Spirit with him. Therefore, let us offer our prayers in the assurance that God remains close to our hearts.

People: Gracious and loving God: By your mercy, help us to lead a life that is holy and acceptable unto you. Comfort us and strengthen us in the good that we try to do. Give success to the work of our hands, and enrichment to our minds. Do not let us be conformed to this world, but let us stand firm in our faith. Even though the wisdom of the cross may seem foolish to the world, we know that it brings your power to save us. We pray in the spirit of Jesus. Amen

Leader: We can be certain of this: Nothing in all of creation will be able to separate us from the love of God in Jesus Christ. Amen

Romans 8:38-39

40. *(For Eastertide)*

Blessed are you, the God and Father of our Lord Jesus Christ. By your great mercy, we have been born anew to a living hope through the resurrection of your Son, the Christ. We hold on to a sure hope and receive the promise of an inheritance which is imperishable and everlasting.

By your power, keep us always in your care, even as we face the trials of life. We rejoice with praise, glory, and honor in the revelation of the risen Christ. For we love him; we believe in him; and we proclaim our joy that his presence abides in us forever. Amen

1 Peter 1:3-9

41. *(For Pentecost)*

Eternal God: It is by the oneness of your Spirit that we have been baptized, but there are many spiritual gifts by which we serve you. Help us to build up your earthly kingdom as each of us, in our own way, adds to its strength and glory.

We rejoice in our diversity, knowing that it creates among us a richer unity. We acknowledge our differences, and yet we come together as one people in the body of Christ.

Empower us through faith, and remind us of our common purposes, that we should grow in all ways into the love and truth of Christ our Lord. Amen

1 Corinthians 12:12-14, 27-31, Ephesians 4:7-16

4

1.   We believe in God, the King of kings and the Lord of lords, who alone is immortal, dwelling in unapproachable light, and has glory, honor, and everlasting power.

We believe in Jesus Christ, whose state was divine, yet did not cling to his equality with God, but emptied himself to become as we are. He was made visible in the flesh, attested by the Spirit, seen by angels, proclaimed to the nations, and taken up in glory.

We believe in the Spirit as a power of the Almighty, a pure emanation of the glory of God. Though unchanging, she makes all things new. She triumphs over evil, and her strength is ever present, ordering all things for good. Amen

1 Timothy 3:14-16 (RSV), Philippians 2:5-7, Wisdom 7:22—8:1

2.   We believe in God the Father, who is the Creator and Redeemer of all the world.

We believe that Jesus Christ is one with the Father, and the works he did in the Father's name were his witness. He was capable of feeling our human weaknesses, but he also ascended to the highest heavens. He was tempted in every way that we are, though he was without sin.

He was obedient through suffering, even suffering unto death. But having been made perfect through suffering, he became the source of our salvation.

We believe that God has given him a name which is above all other names, that at the name of Jesus, every knee should bow in heaven and on earth, and every tongue confess, that Jesus Christ is Lord, to the glory of God the Father. Amen

John 10:25, Hebrews 4:14—5:9, Philippians 2:9-11 (RSV)

3.   We believe that God created the universe, which stands firmly in his glory. He is from everlasting to everlasting.

We believe in Jesus Christ, who is the image of the unseen God; the first born of all creation; the Word made flesh who dwelt among us, full of grace and truth. We have beheld his glory, glory as of the only Son from the Father.

We believe in the Holy Spirit, the eternal light of God and a reflection of his power in the world. By the work of the Spirit, we are transformed into the likeness of God and claimed as his own, for the glory of his Kingdom. Amen

Colossians 1:15, John 1:14 (RSV), 2 Corinthians 3:17-18

4.   We believe in God, our Creator and Redeemer, whose rule is over all the earth.

We believe that by his infinite power, God raised his Son, Jesus Christ, to new life; and Christ ascended into heaven, far above every power, dominion, and authority, both in this age and in the age to come.

We believe that the church is founded upon the resurrection of Christ. He is the head of the church and we are the body. Christ calls us to be his disciples, and to proclaim our faith among all the nations, to the glory of God almighty. Amen

Ephesians 1:19-23 (RSV), Romans 1:1-7

5.   We believe in God the Father, who is the Lord of life and the Creator of the world, and the work of creation is full of his glory.

We believe in Jesus Christ, who dwelt among us, and experienced death for all humanity, so that we could share in God's glory.

We believe in the power of the Holy Spirit, by which the love of God dwells within us, and our faith in God will make its own power felt through love.

We believe that the church is a spiritual community, founded in Christ, to serve God and the whole human family.

We believe in the Kingdom of God, both in this world and in the world to come, and this Kingdom is from everlasting to everlasting. Amen

Hebrews 2:9-11, Romans 5:1-5

6. We believe that God is love, and his love was perfectly revealed to us when he sent his Son, Jesus Christ, into the world.

We believe that God destined his Son to be the Savior of all humankind, by making him the pure and sufficient sacrifice that took away our sins and restored us to wholeness.

We believe that God dwells within us by the power of the Holy Spirit. And within the community of the Spirit, God calls us to be the church of Jesus Christ, and to love and serve one another for his name's sake. Amen

1 John 3:22—4:12

7. We believe in the living God, who endures forever; who works signs and wonders in heaven and on earth; and whose kingdom shall never pass away.

We believe in Jesus Christ, who was resurrected from the dead and proclaimed the Son of God in all his power, according to the Spirit of holiness within him.

We believe that as God raised the Lord Jesus to new life, so also will he renew us by the Spirit dwelling within us. For the Spirit bears us witness that we belong to God and share in his glory, both now and forever more. Amen

Daniel 6:26-27, 7:14 (RSV), Romans 1:4, 8:9-16

8.   We believe in God the Father, who is the source of wisdom, power, love, honor, glory, and blessing.

We believe in the Son of God, who revealed to us the fulness of divinity and the perfection of humanity. God has made him both Lord and Christ, and has put all things under his feet.

We believe that the church is the body of Christ, and represents the completion of him who fulfills everything within creation. Our witness to Christ is this: that God has given us eternal life, and this life is in his Son. Amen

Revelations 5:13, Ephesians 1:19-23, Acts 2:36, 1 John 5:11

9.   We believe in God, who created the heavens and the earth; who made all things and called them good.

We believe in Jesus Christ, who came from above and is above all others; who was born of the earth and belongs to it; who bears witness to the truth of God, because God has given all things into his hand.

We believe that God brings us into union with Christ by putting the seal of his Holy Spirit within our hearts. All of us together form one body in Christ, and we are called to serve one another through faith and discipleship to the glory of his name. Amen

Genesis 1, John 3:31-36, 2 Corinthians 1:21-22, Romans 12:4-5,16

10. *Leader:* This is the commandment we have received: that
         we love one another as God has loved us.
    People: **We love, because God first loved us.**
    Leader: Everyone who loves is born of God and knows
         God;
    People: **And whoever fails to love does not know God.**
    Leader: For love is of God,

People: **And his love will be made complete in us.**

Leader: We know that God abides in us and we in him, because of the testimony of his Spirit.

People: **We ourselves testify that the Father sent his Son as the Savior of the world.**

Leader: And God's love was revealed in Christ;

People: **That in him, we would live in love and have the light of life. Amen**

1 John 4

5

1.   We praise you, O God, for the spirit of our humanity and the goodness of the earth. As we go about our daily living, we see the evidences of your creating power and sustaining love. You have provided us with bread for the body and light for the soul.

   We thank you for guiding us through difficult situations, for upholding us during times of illness, and for steering us away from the sources of destruction and harm.

   Of all the joys that fill each day, we know that you are their ultimate source. Enable us to spread your joy among others and proclaim your presence in the midst of our world.

   Send forth your Spirit, O God, and kindle the fire of love within us. Wherever the Spirit may lead us, let us go, even if we must take the risk of being hurt or rejected. We cannot ask to be perfect, but we can be faithful.

   We worship you through the nearness of your Son, the Christ, who is life to the living, hope to the dying, and unending peace to all who seek him. In his name, we offer you our thanks and praise. Amen

2.   O God of light: Free us from the shadows of doubt and the darkness of despair. Help us to see the miracles of this world, and know that you are the author of all good things.

   O God of mercy: We sometimes feel guilty for our many shortcomings. We want to be better people. We want to complete all those tasks that go undone, and say all the words that go unspoken. Remind us of our worthiness to you and to one another, and restore us to a sense of wholeness.

O God of peace: Let your Spirit dwell within our homes and places of work. Let it spread across the earth and fill the troubled places of our world. Help us to love as you have loved, and give us the courage of our convictions, that we might speak out against whatever is wrong and unjust.

O God of beauty: We praise you for the flowers that bloom in the ghetto; for a child's laughter that breaks the silence of loneliness; for the changing of seasons which reminds us that life is in transition.

O God of every god: To be a part of your creation is to know that there is a time and a place for every matter under heaven. Let us rejoice in the life you have given us, and let us strive to uphold your kingdom in which we dwell. Grant us your grace, your goodness, and your power. Amen

3.   We thank you, O God, for the quietness of prayer. It brings us peace within ourselves and peace with one another.

At times, the world may seem to us a struggle, and yet there are acts of kindness shown to us each day. We know that others care for us and help us along our life's journey.

Surely Christ is there. For he makes his presence and power known, and we see in him the divine source of our being and all our doing. Help us to receive his way, his truth, and his life into our hearts. As he so taught us, we do not live unto ourselves, but we are able to discover the joy of obedience to your will and the fulfillment of sacrificing for others.

Whenever we fail to follow commandments, O God, and we mostly certainly do, remind us that we are forgiven, healed, and restored to the newness of life, with all its fresh possibilities.

Help us to accept the things of our past, and not be ashamed. Enable us to embrace the present with insight, enthusiasm, and purpose. Empower us to look to the future with confidence and hope. In the fellowship of your Holy Spirit, we pray these things together. Amen

4. *Prayer of Intercession (Follow each sentence by a period of silence.)*

God of grace and compassion: You hear us in our silence as well as our words,

> so hear us as we pray for those we love . . .

> we pray for those who suffer from illness or disability. . .

> we pray for all who are troubled in spirit or troubled by circumstance . . .

> we pray for the family, that it may be affirmed and nurtured in our society . . .

> we pray for people all over the world who live under a cloud of oppression . . .

> we pray for the beauty of the earth . . .

> Hear our prayers, O Lord, and grant us your peace. Amen

5.   O Lord our God: How great is your name upon all the earth. Your majesty is praised above the heavens, upon the lips of those who love you and seek your grace.

You gave power to your Son, the Christ, within the order of creation, so that we would be reconciled unto you. He is the Word made flesh, dwelling among us in spirit and truth, and his power to save is utterly certain.

When we look upon the heavens, the moon, and the stars, which you have established, who are we that you should care for us and remember us in our need? You have made us with a spark of divinity so that we can share in your many blessings. You have given us dominion over the earth and all the works of your hands, in order to accomplish your good.

O Lord, our God, your greatness is unsearchable. Let this generation praise your works to another, as all of creation speaks of your glory and tells of your kingdom which endures forever. Amen

Psalm 8, John 1:14

6.   We are in prayer, O God, as your Spirit dwells within us, in all its peace and calmness.

The world outside is busy. There is traffic on the streets. Stores are getting ready to open their doors. Everywhere, there are sights and sounds of people starting a new day, in whatever way they may choose.

But we are here; and we thank you for this place of worship which brings us rest and reflection. It is here that we feel the sorrows of the world, and look forward to the opportunities awaiting us.

Outside, people are searching for food, seeking a job, looking for a place to sleep. There are people in prison, people in exile, people suffering in every imaginable way. There are some families fighting with each other. There are some people who will not make it through the day without another drink or another pill.

There is much of life that we do not understand. We do not know why some people experience more misfortune than others. But we pray that all of our lives will hold more good than ill, and that we will be drawn toward hope rather than hopelessness.

This is why we pray, O God. Indeed, you have drawn us here to do so. Help us to be uplifting in our attitudes, and strengthen us for your work in the world, so that we may serve you along all the paths that we walk, in all the ways that we labor, and among all the people whom we love. Amen

7.   God of wisdom and understanding: We search for appropriate words to say as we come to you in prayer. When words fail us, let us speak to you through our silence, knowing that you hear us at all times and in all places.

Our lives are filled with so many wants, that we often forget how you provide for our needs. Show us the joy of simplicity, and help us to grow in our appreciation for the basic goodness of life: for the caring of friends, the love of family, the familiarity of home and community, the freshness of morning and the quiet of night, the cry of a newborn baby and a mother's warm embrace. Everywhere we turn, we find the marks of our Creator.

Help us to accept the part of life which is mysterious and unknowable. Give us the fortitude to cope with our failures and to accept our limitations. We are what we are, and in each one of us, you have endowed a beauty, a dignity, and a reason for our being.

We pray for the gifts of the Spirit: for peace, patience, goodness, love, joy, and faithfulness. By these qualities, let us grow unto your likeness, according to the example of Christ our Lord.

You are the God who guides us. You alone know the glory within us. We will hold on to our hopes and strive toward our dreams, because you are with us always. For this, we give you our thanks and praise. Amen

Galatians 5:22

8.   O God, our strength and refuge: You have seen our trouble and sorrow, and you take it upon your hands to give us comfort in time of need. We know whoever feels helpless can turn to you, for indeed, you are the helper of all.

Your power stretches across the earth, and yet you rule over each one of us with gentleness and compassion. Your mercy reaches to the heavens, your truth to the skies. Your justice is like a mountain, and your wisdom like the deep. You are the source of life and love.

Teach us your ways, O God, that we may act with kindness and witness to your message of hope. We remember that Christ came into the world to break down the barriers that divide us. He brought new life into our hearts so that hostility might die within us. He is the peace among us and the peace within us.

We thank you for the beauty of nature: its order, its harmony, and its colors. We see about us also, the wonder of our own humanity. Help us to aspire toward our noblest virtues of integrity, humility, and love.

Let us always be one in the Spirit, O God, reconciled to you and one another. Send your blessings upon those who are far away and those who are near at hand. Let us all discover the joy that this life has to offer us according to the promises of your word, through Jesus Christ our Lord. Amen

Psalm 36:5-6

9.   Gracious and loving God: Our prayers reach out today
to all who are in need of your healing power.
    We pray for those who suffer from debilitating dis-
eases. Give them courage to hold on to the goodness of
life, even in the face of despair. We know that you have
a purpose for each one of us within your plan for creation, so let us affirm the importance of every life, regard-
less of circumstance, and remind us that we all live by your
mercy and grace.
    We pray for those who seek healing from broken rela-
tionships. Give strength to those who have gone through
the anguish of divorce and other conflicts of relationship.
Bring comfort to those who have lost a loved one, and
fill the empty spaces of their lives with peace. Remind us
that to live is to love, even if to love means having to lose.
    We pray for all those who seek healing of the human
spirit. Let your light shine upon those who struggle through
deep doubts and depression. Free us all from the burdens
which we bring with us today: feelings of anger, jealousy,
fear, lust, or greed. Protect the health of our soul, O God,
and remove all the obstacles which prevent us from being
closer to you.
    Your love breaks in upon us when we least expect it,
for some of us feel as if we have reached the end of our
strength. But you are in our midst to sustain us, and by
your power, you will wipe away every tear from our eyes.
Help us to love life as much as you have loved us, and
we will return our praise to the glory of your name. Amen

10.   Almighty God: We are the clay; you are the potter.
We are all the work of your hands. Your love is eternal
and your wisdom is beyond measure.
    Though the grass withers and the flower fades, your
Word will stand forever. It is a lamp unto our steps and

a light for our path as we walk along our earthly ways.

Help us to walk together as a community of faith, knowing that our joys and hurts are no longer our own, but are shared within this fellowship of your Spirit. If ever we are sorrowful, surely you can turn our sorrow into gladness; and in our receiving it, no one can take it from us.

Let us feel the strength and energy which flow from our worship, and let this spiritual force transform not only our own lives but the world around us.

We live in the assurance that there is nothing which will ever defeat us, so long as we hold the Christ within our hearts. Help us to be rooted in him, built on him, and held firm in the faith we have in him.

Let us go forward from this day with perseverance and hope, knowing that your goodness and grace will fulfill our every need. Amen

Isaiah 64:8, Psalm 25:4-5, Psalm 119:105, John 16:20, 23

11. *Prayer of Intercession (Follow each sentence by a period of silence.)*

Let us be in silence and in prayer with God.

Dear God: We pray for the integrity of our relationships . . .

Help us to feel forgiveness where we have refused to be forgiving . . .

We ask that you take away the anxieties and fears which burden us, and make us free again . . .

We pray for a pure heart and a clear mind in a world of moral confusion . . .

We pray for the leaders of our nation and of all nations . . .

We pray for the church as it stands boldly in the world . . .

Dear God, grant us wisdom, patience, goodness, love, joy, peace. Amen

12.   O God, who knows us in our resting and our rising: All our ways lie open to you. You discern our purposes from afar. You know our innermost thoughts and the secrets that are deep within our hearts. You hear our words even before they are spoken.

Your wisdom is so high, so wonderful, that we cannot attain it; but we know that your favor is upon us. You have brought us into being, and you guide us through the nearness of your Spirit. The darkness cannot hide us from you, for by your mercy even the night is as light as day.

There is nowhere that we can go from your Spirit, for indeed, you will never forsake us. If we were to climb the highest mountain, you would be there. If we were to dwell in the uttermost parts of the sea, you also would be there.

You have loved us with an everlasting love, and have been constant in your affection for us. Help us to walk with ever-growing strength, knowing that our happiness will always be found in you. Amen

Psalm 139, Jeremiah 31:1-7

13.   We are truly one people in you, O God, though it often seems otherwise in the ways of our world. We come to this sanctuary today, aware of the turmoils surrounding us, but we also come seeking a peace for our world and

within our souls.

Give us a mind of wisdom and a heart of faith as we cope with the struggles of our time. We see nations embroiled in war; we see people whose basic needs go unfulfilled; we see the cause of freedom being stifled. Dear God, let your justice roll down like waters, and your righteousness like an ever-flowing stream. Make your presence and power known to all who strive for human dignity and wholeness.

You have called us to be citizens of the world and the children of God. Help us to do away with the clenched fist and the evil word. Enable us to rise above all our competing loyalties, and seek the deeper bond of our common humanity. For the love which you have taught us is kind and compassionate, and knows no boundaries.

We are indeed our brothers' and sisters' keepers, as Christ taught us that whatsoever we do unto one another, we do so unto him. So let us look for the Christ within each of us, and remember his commandment to love as he has loved us. Amen

Amos 5:24 (RSV), Matthew 25:40

14.   O God of the universe: We thank you for the wonder of your creation, where even the sparrow finds a home. We rejoice to see life bringing forth new life and all the possibilities for growth and renewal. Let us be aware of the creative spirit which you have put into each one of us.

O God of mercy: Grant us your forgiving love. We have failed to live up to the demands of the Gospel, even though they bring us freedom and fulfillment. You alone know how wide a gap there is between what we do and what we intend to do, so enable us to live in greater faithfulness and obedience to your word.

O God of compassion: Be with us in our times of need. We pray for the lonely, the brokenhearted, those who are ill, and those who are troubled in mind and spirit. Give strength to the wearied, and uphold the powerless. Keep us all under the shadow of your wing.

O God of everlasting goodness: We thank you for the special blessings of family, home, and community; and for your church and the presence of your Spirit, which guides us in the ways of Christ. As we remember the sacrifice that Christ made on our behalf, let us respond with a loving heart and a helping hand toward others.

We will leave this place of worship today to go into the world as a people of faith. But let us also return here, knowing that we have walked beside you and that you have cared for us as your own. Amen

15.   Dear Heavenly Father: We come before you in prayer, not always knowing what to say or how to say it, but trusting in your power to hear us. We give thanks for the presence of your Spirit, which sustains us in all that we do.

We realize that every day does not bring contentment, and every challenge does not find fulfillment, but you have called us to live by faith rather than despair.

As we look upon the grace of our Lord Jesus Christ, let us see within ourselves a capacity for goodness and virtue. Help us to discover the very best within us, and give us courage to engage in the great adventure of living.

By the unity of your Spirit, O God, you have called us together in the whole family of humankind. Remind us of our ability to love and be loved, so that we may reflect a measure of your inexhaustible love.

As each of us strive toward the heights of our potential, we know that you are with us not only in our success and in our failure, but you are also with us in our striving.

May your will be done in us, and among all those who love you. Amen

16. *Prayer of Intercession (Follow each sentence by a period of silence.)*

In our stillness, we know that you are God. You hear us through our speaking, our doing, and our very being. Be with us now as we lift up our concerns in prayer.

We pray for the peace of our world . . .

We pray for nations struggling with hunger, poverty, and disease . . .

We pray for all those who are in crisis or with some special need . . .

We pray for the dignity of human life and the labors of our love . . .

We pray for the fulfillment of our hopes and dreams . . .

We pray that the power of the Holy Spirit may come upon us . . .

Dear God, grant us your mercy, your grace, and your peace. Amen

17.   We thank you, O God, for the peace and tranquillity of prayer. It gives us pause from the busyness of life, and enables us to reflect upon who we are and what we can become.

Jesus taught us that when we pray, you already know what we need before we ask you. So we seek most of all to feel your closeness and to live with confidence in your Word. Give us the insight to know our true needs and the courage to find their fulfillment in you.

You have made us in your image and you have blessed us with a spark of divinity that ignites the thoughts of our minds and touches the depths of our souls. It is a spark that leads us in your path. It gives us hope when everything else has failed, and it breaks through the barriers that hide our secret fears and pain. You have brought us healing in the midst of broken dreams, broken promises, and broken lives.

We praise you for the Christ, who was triumphant through love. He shared in our humanness; he felt our sufferings; he conquered the limitations of our world. Help us to serve one another as Christ has served us, and fill us with his grace. Let us proclaim his kingdom on earth, and live in the light of his redeeming love. We pray in his name. Amen

18.   Almighty and everlasting God: We pray to you out of pain whenever we encounter frustration, disappointment, and loss. We know that your will for the world is not always the same as our own. Help us to accept adversity, even with reluctant hearts, so that we may transform our misfortunes into opportunity.

We pray to you out of faith that evil will be judged and righteousness exalted. Though we may struggle through times of uncertainty, we trust that you will make your blessings known. Let us wait in quietness and listen for your word, for your help is near to all who believe in your name.

We pray to you with hope, that even in the midst of

the world's troubles, we would still see the possibilities for change. Give light to those who live in darkness, and guide us all in the ways of peace.

We pray to you with joy, giving thanks for the ties that bind us to the whole human family, and for the deepest expressions of love which we share with one another. You have not put us into this world to be alone, and so we are grateful for those who uphold us in all that we are and in all that we do.

Make us faithful witnesses to all your blessings upon our world, so that others may join us in working toward your good and in building up your kingdom upon the earth. Amen

19.   O Lord our God: How great is your creation over all the world, clothed in splendor and wrapped in light. You have established the earth to stand firm from age to age, and you have shaped it with mountains and plains. You make springs to flow through the valleys and between the hills; and along their banks dwell the birds of air as they sing with joy. How great are your works, O God, for in wisdom, you have made them all.

We thank you for your Son, the Christ, who walked among us a fellow human being; who resisted temptation and overcame the voices of fear and intimidation. He is truly the light of the world and the promise of our salvation. Let us open our hearts and minds to receive the teachings of Christ and appropriate them to our living. Let us remember the ways in which he ministered unto others, sometimes by no more than the touch of his hand. We trust that Christ is calling us to the same ministry, according to the examples he has set before us.

Dear God, your love has shined upon us at times when we have least expected it. You have been the source of our

comfort and the foundation of our hope. You accept us
for who we are, and at the same time, you place great ex-
pectations upon us. Help us to live boldly in the world,
so that we may appreciate all the gifts of our humanity,
and know the fulness of your love. Amen

Psalm 104

20.   Creator God, who ordained our birth and the origins
of all things: We praise you for your everlasting goodness,
and we ask that you guide us in the ways of righteousness. Just as the earth makes fresh things grow, and a
garden brings forth new seed, so let faithfulness blossom
and grow in us. And may others see in us the witness of
our faith so that they too, will believe.

There are times when we have all known misfortune,
but you give us peace to balance our affliction. We pray
for all those who bring with them special concerns today:
(Follow each sentence by a period of silence.)

We pray for those who are hospitalized or confined
to home . . .
We pray for those who have recently lost a loved one
. . .
We pray for people whose jobs bring them a great
amount of stress or conflict . . .
We pray for young people who are searching for the
right values to live by . . .
And we pray for all those who are in need of your hope,
that they may not call this a hopeless world . . .

Dear God, send your mercy upon all who seek you.
May your Spirit cóme alive in each one of us and fill us
with the glory of your presence. We do not belong to the
night or the darkness, but we live according to the light
of your love. You are the God who saves us, and in you
our hearts rejoice now and forever more. Amen

Isaiah 6:11

21.   Eternal God: As we come to this sanctuary to offer our praise, we thank you for your peace, your quiet, your comfort, and your safety. Surely you restore our soul and uplift our spirit.

Yet the images of the world outside remain in our thoughts. We see the images of . . . *(mention some current events/people here)*

We pray to you as the Lord of life and ask that you restore our world according to your plan for creation. Move us beyond our attachment to race, culture, and nationality, and give us a sense of belonging to the whole human family. Make us all more loving, more caring, more aware of the needs of others.

We thank you for the hope that fills our lives, and for all the possibilities we have for new journeys and discoveries along the paths that we walk. We know that Christ is with us, and that his spirit dwells within us. By his love, let us be assured of our worthiness to the whole of your kingdom. You have given each of us a portion of life which is uniquely our own, and as we share that part of life with one another, we are thankful for the wonderful mixture of our humanity. Let us see the beauty in every face and feel the warmth which comes from every heart, and there we shall find you also. Amen

22.   God of grace and author of eternal love: You are the help of all who call upon your name, for you dwell in every time and place.

We come to you in prayer with our own special needs. Some of us have experienced deep disappointments. Some of us have known suffering in our lives or we have seen it in those close to us. Others of us feel anxious about decisions we have to make or obligations we must meet. And all these things lie deep within our hearts, awaiting new direction and resolution. So fill us with your wisdom and empower us for the challenges which lie ahead.

As we go about our daily living, we look for the signs of faith in our world. We pray that your presence would be felt in the ways that we conduct our business and commerce, and in the ways that we govern our community and nation. We want to see good triumph over evil, and righteousness vindicated. Let us be confident and have patience in the working out of your justice, for our sorrow may be only a moment, but our joy will last a lifetime.

Remind us of the example of Christ, the one who remained authentically human against the forces of destruction. We too, live in the same kind of world where we hear voices among us making false promises and promoting false values; and though we are inclined to reject them, we ask for the inner strength to do so. Help us to overcome whatever stands in our way of becoming a people of God. Keep us ever in your care and assure us of your saving power through Jesus Christ, our Lord. Amen

23.   God of all goodness and power: You know us by name, for you have called each one of us into being. As we pray, we are reminded of your close presence and the compassion which you have shown to all who seek your help.

Sometimes we want to live in the world as if we were always bold and self-assured, but we realize how fragile and vulnerable we are as human beings. Our feelings are easily hurt; we dwell on our failures much more than our successes; we feel the limitations of our time and energy keeping us from doing all that we want to do. But remind us that our measure of a worthy life is not always the same as yours. Let us look to the designs of your creation, and there we will find our true humanity.

As we pray for the health of our own soul, let us also keep before us the critical needs of all your people. Help us to give comfort to the afflicted and acceptance to the outcast according to your tender mercy. Create in us a loving spirit that will transcend our limited vision. Lift our sights higher and higher until we find our place of belonging within the whole family of God, and there we will discover that we are all brothers and sisters.

All across the earth, let the wind whisper peace: a peace within us, a peace among us; a peace that surpasses all our understanding. Lead us to this hope, O God, and in our finding it, let us be grateful. Amen

24. *Prayer of Intercession (Follow each sentence by a period of silence.)*

In our silence, let us be in prayer.

Let us pray for those we love . . .

Let us pray for those who are unloved . . .

Let us pray for this church and all the possibilities awaiting us for ministry, and outreach, and making disciples . . .

Let us pray for the needs of our community . . .

Let us pray for the soul of our nation . . .

Pray for me and I will pray for you . . .

Let the church say together: Amen.

25.   God of amazing grace: Your power is at work over

all the earth, in every part of your creation, and within each one of us. You call us to rise above all selfish desires and live harmoniously with nature, in family and community, and among all the peoples of the world. Remind us of our heavenly image and our capacity for good, as we draw from the source of your eternal goodness.

We thank you for the many qualities with which you have endowed our humanity. We thank you for our capacities to be healed of diseases; to experience the senses of touch, sight, sound, and smell; to express ourselves as male and female; to be creative, each in our own way; and to be attached to the earth and feel the rhythms of time and season. In all these ways, O God, we are grateful for the gift of life.

Help us to strive toward the goals which are within our reach. For sometimes we admit that we are more comfortable in seeking security rather than taking risks. We often prefer the small scope of our familiarities instead of opening ourselves up to new people and new situations. How much easier it is for us never to try than to say, "I tried and I failed."

Let your Spirit push us onward, O God, challenging us to look not at what is, but what might be. Sustain us in all that we do, for you have shown us the way, and the truth and the life, through our Lord Jesus Christ, in whose name we pray. Amen

26.   Almighty God, Creator and Preserver of all humankind, the author of everlasting grace: We who live in the shadow of worldly powers, are reminded that you alone are the source of our strength and security. As we have heard, so we have seen, the glories of your justice and might. We ponder your love in the midst of this sanctuary where you dwell, and we thank you for the peace

of your close presence. Let all the peoples of the world remember your many blessings, and let the mighty of the earth bow down in humbleness.

We remember your mighty works of old, and we give thanks for the Scriptures which tell of your faithfulness to all generations. You are, indeed, the God who works wonders. We thank you for the covenant which you established through Abraham, Isaac, and Jacob; for the commandments which you gave through Moses; and for the gift of your Son, the Christ, who came into the world to assure us that we shall not perish, but have life eternal. With this faith we have inherited, O God, let us find our own place of belonging within the Scriptures.

We think of the example of the disciples, who were ordinary people going about their ordinary tasks when they became the followers of Christ. May we find our own sense of calling and purpose as we go about our daily tasks and strive to serve you in the world. Let us be the messengers of your truth not only in what we proclaim, but also by how we live. Breath into us the power of your Holy Spirit, and make us pure in heart, for we are all the work of your hands. Amen

Psalm 48, John 3:16

27.   God of light and love: Through the grandeur and beauty of every living thing, we contemplate you as the author of creation. Your glory dwells in our land, and the earth yields its fruit. We praise your name together, and let all who hear us be glad.

Help us to see your love for all people, so that we may become more loving ourselves. And help us to be more understanding of human weakness, for we know that through the power of Christ, all things shall be made equal. As you bring comfort to those who are in need, let us be your messengers of good will.

We thank you for people of great vision and compassion: those who cure deadly diseases and touch the untouchable; those who are imprisoned for matters of conscience; and those who dare to explore the universe. So too, in all of our endeavors, let us join with one another to awaken new dimensions of the human spirit as we come into touch with the power of your Holy Spirit. Help us to hold on to our high ideals, our sense of mission to the world, and to all the dreams which stir in our hearts and long to find fulfillment in you.

We thank you for the church which is built upon the foundation of our living Lord, and which calls each one of us to build upon that foundation by our faithful witness. May your love reach to the depths of our soul, reminding us that even now, we are part of your kingdom, because your kingdom dwells within us. Amen

28.   Most merciful God: In our gathering together as a community of faith, we see faces among us which hide the anguish that is felt inside, for all of us have our own stories to tell. So we lift up in prayer all the needs that are known to us and those which are unknown, and ask that you take them unto yourself with your saving power.

Remind us of how sin brings about our separation, as we find a sense of divisiveness among nations, and races, and religions in the world. We may even find it within our own families; and all of us have experienced a divided self as our actions become separated from the intentions of our heart. Help us to bring together all the fragmentations of our lives, and make us whole again. For you have shown us what is good, O God, so let us seek to do your justice, to love kindness, and to walk humbly with you.

Help us to endure all the hardships that befall us, and find strength in our moments of weakness, for this is how the Power of Christ comes upon us. We wish that personal growth were not born out of pain, nor love out of sacrifice. We wish that reconciliation could be accomplished without struggle and compromise, but you call upon us to bear the costs of living out a genuine faith.

Help us to hold on to all that is worthy and find contentment within our souls. We know that ultimately, our yoke is easy and our burden is light, because of Christ, who has enabled us to live anew according to your love. Amen

Micah 6:8

29.   How great and wonderful are all your works, O God of wisdom, power, and love. Justice marches before you, and peace follows in your steps. We praise your name together, for you alone are holy.

You care for us as you have cared for all of your creation, and you are the source of our hope and deliverance. Though we may cry through the night, surely there is joy by day. All of us have known sorrow; we have endured the pain of adversity and rejection; our bodies have felt the weakness of distress. But there is no need for us to flee from our problems, our conflicts, and our fears, for we put our trust in you. If ever we should suffer, let it be for doing right instead of wrong, and we will find our vindication in you as the author of righteousness.

You have restored us to new life in Christ, and have made his presence known in all times and places. Teach us in his ways, so that we too, may have the qualities of humbleness, gentleness, and compassion.

O Lord, our God, for your name's sake, preserve us in faithfulness, and keep us true to the love which we feel for you and for one another. May our lips tell of your wonders, and day by day of your help, as we live in the assurance of your many blessings upon us. Amen

Revelation 15:3-4, Psalm 85:13, Psalm 30:5, 1 Peter 3:17

30. *(For Advent)*

O God of heavenly light: We remember that the hope of the world came to us in a child. And that event, in its quietness and simplicity, draws us to you in prayer. We rejoice in the Christ child, and we are reminded that you have called us to be your children as well.

We thank you for the joy of this season; for the love of family and the warmth of home; for the celebration of worship and the inspiration of music; and for the peace of Christ which surpasses all our understanding.

Keep us strong in your Spirit, O God. Let us rejoice in doing your will. We pray that the truth of your word will be felt upon our world, and that you will guide us in all the important decisions which affect our future.

We see about us the struggle for human rights and the basic necessities of life. Let us share in those struggles to relieve the world's sorrows and be joined to our fellow humanity.

Just as wise men made their journey to Bethlehem, we too, begin a journey of faith. We sometimes falter and fail; we are aware of our limitations, our hurts, and our anxieties; but ultimately, we will find our own place of belonging beside the manger.

The light that shined out of darkness is a light for all the world to see. Let us be born anew in this hope, as we receive Christ into our hearts. He is the King of kings and the Lord of lords, and to him we return all honor, glory, and blessing, now and forever more. Amen

31. *(For Advent)*

We give thanks, O God, for this season of Advent and our anticipation of Christmas morning. Many of us will have the occasion to gather with friends or reunite with family. But it may also be a time which intensifies the hurts and losses which we have endured over the years. We recall the memories of Christmases past.

We remember those whom we have loved and lost, and surely we miss them for their warmth, their laughter, and their close presence. Some of us will struggle to celebrate Christmas in the midst of a divided family. And others of us will feel the emptiness of being many miles away from those we love.

In spite of the sorrows we may feel, let us be uplifted by your hope and filled with your joy. As your disciples, let us minister unto others and bring comfort to the troubles of their heart.

May this be more than a time of celebration for us, but also an opportunity to experience anew your spiritual power. As we behold the beauty of the Christ child, let us find within ourselves the measure of godliness which you have bestowed upon us.

You have shown us your mercy, O God, in taking away the sins of the world, and in wiping away every tear from our eyes. You are the God in whom we have longed for our salvation, and now you bring your promise into being with the giving of your Son. Let us rejoice in his name, and seek our fulfillment in him. Amen

32. *(For Advent)*

Almighty God: We thank you for the reflection of prayer as we ponder anew the coming of your Son, the Christ. We wait to hear the babe crying so that we may respond in faith. And in our responding, we realize that it is we who need him, rather than he who needs us.

We hail the Prince of Peace, the King of kings, who comes into our world to dwell among the nations and all our peoples. Though much divides us, let us find unity through him and come to an understanding of our common humanity.

Bring peace to each of us, so that we may find contentment in our labors and harmony within our relationships. As you have sent your Son to assure us of your unconditional love and acceptance, may we also be so loving and accepting of others.

What brought shepherds and wise men to the awareness of a bright hope and a new destiny is what leads us toward the same promise. Let us prepare ourselves through faith to share in the great joy of Christ's birth, and behold it in all its glory; for we, too, are part of the Christmas story. Let this great joy live within our hearts and for all generations to come. Amen

33. *(For Advent)*

Dear Heavenly Father: Our lives are filled with expectation as we await the coming of your Son. In this season which is filled with so many gifts, let us not forget the greatest gifts of life that touch our hearts and deepen the spirit within us.

We thank you most of all for the gift of your Savior to the world. Though he came to us in humbleness and lowliness, he has been crowned the King of Glory. He has shown us the purpose for our being and our destiny in him.

We thank you for the gift of human love, which draws us together in family and friendship. Let this love which we feel for one another move us in charity toward all those who are in need. For Christ came into the world to seek and to save the lost.

We thank you for the gift of faith and for the community of believers. Bless this church in the celebration of our worship and in our service unto others. We thank you for the warmth of our fellowship and for the many ways in which we strive to further your kingdom on earth.

We give thanks, O God, for the gift of hope. As we encounter all of life's struggles, we look for the shining star to lead us out of darkness and into your light.

These are the gifts of Christmas which you have entrusted to us so that we may proclaim them to the world. By your power, make us the givers of every good and perfect gift which comes from you. Amen

Luke 19:10

34. *(For Christmas)*

Gracious God our Father, who by a shining star guided shepherds to behold your Son, our Lord: Show unto us your heavenly light, and give us grace to follow that star until we find him, and in finding him, rejoice.

Just as wise men knelt before the manger with precious gifts, we now bring to you our offerings of a loving heart, an obedient will, and a joyful spirit.

As we share at Christmas time the giving and receiving of gifts, let us remember what our gifts are meant to express: that we cherish the love of family; treasure our friendships; appreciate the kindnesses and support of neighbors and co-workers; and value our Christian fellowship with one another.

We thank you for this church, which lives and breathes the spirit of Christmas throughout the year. You have empowered us for ministry, and you have called us to serve the needs of our community and world.

We pray that the living Christ will enter the lives of each one of us here, enabling us to love you more perfectly, and to reflect an image of your heavenly will.

Dear God, do not let the light of Christmas fade with a flickering candle flame, but let it shine within our hearts both now and forever more. We pray these things to the glory of your name and in Christ Jesus our Lord. Amen

35. *(For Lent)*

Strengthen us, O God, as we walk in the paths of our integrity. We believe in ourselves because we believe in you. There are many struggles that we encounter in life. Help us to confront them with courage and confidence, knowing that you are near in our moments of need.

We bring to you, O God, the sorrows of the world and the sorrows of our hearts, and we pour them out to you because you share in our burdens. Free us from any sense of guilt or failure that we hold within us, so that we may live with greater resolve toward accomplishing your will.

We gratefully receive the many blessings of this life, and we are challenged to find even the blessings in disguise. Empower us to transform defeat into opportunity, darkness into light, and suffering into hope. And we ask for this power through Christ, who transformed even death into life.

By the promise of the resurrection we find our sense of belonging not only to your kingdom upon earth, but also to your kingdom above. You are the God who can do all things. We will tell of your name to the next generation, and we will proclaim your love and mercy even to a people yet unborn. May others see in us the grace you have given us, and may we grow unto the likeness of our Lord Jesus Christ. Amen

36. *(For Lent)*

O God, who is with us in all our life's journeys: We lift up our hearts unto you as the source of our creation and our help in every time of need. We await new adventures before us, and we give thanks for opportunities fulfilled. You have blessed us with the memories of times gone by, and you point us toward a future that is full of promise.

Though we still encounter the trials of life, you, O Lord, remain our keeper. You know the fears we combat, the temptations we resist, and the limitations we must overcome. We live in the assurance that you will free us from all evil, and preserve our lives according to your faithfulness.

For the sake of your kingdom, help us to seek your good for the world, and serve one another in the fellowship of your Spirit. Remind us of the many human needs which are never met and of the struggles among so many people in the world for freedom and justice. Let your compassion be upon all who feel suffering and sorrow.

We thank you, O God, for your abiding presence, and for sending your Son, the Christ, to dwell among us. He has shown us the qualities of goodness, mercy, wisdom, and love. He is like a tree that is planted beside the living waters, whose leaf does not wither, because in all that he does, he will prosper. He has revealed to us the hope and the destiny that we have in him, and together we rejoice in his name. Amen

Psalm 1:3

37. *(For Lent)*

Almighty God: We await the glory of Easter with great anticipation. For in the life, death, and resurrection of Christ, we find the hope of our salvation. But let us do more than wait. Show us how we may respond to your gospel message. We know that there is nothing we can do to earn your love, but by our actions, we can show how your love is revealed through us.

We remember the words of Paul, how he said that we were bought with a price, and that price was the suffering and death of Christ upon the cross. We are grateful for the gift of eternal life, as it has been promised unto us, and for the assurance that the goodness of the heavens and the earth will conquer all evil.

In our love for Christ, help us to know him not as an historical figure who belongs to the past, but as the living Lord who rules over our world and who lives within our hearts. Indeed, his presence is real; his love is everlasting; and his kingdom will endure forever.

Let us look for the Christ in every person and show the same love and caring for others that has been shown unto us. Make us more worshipful through our daily lives so that we may have a sense of fulfilling your will in everything we do.

We thank you for the church, which exists in the world as a visible presence of the body of Christ. Let us draw upon the spiritual power of Christ as it works in and through the church and so empowers each one of us. Make us your living witnesses in the world through the ways that we serve you and in the faith that we proclaim. Amen

1 Corinthians 6:20

38. *(For Palm Sunday)*

We remember the palms, dear God, as we recall that Christ was not utterly rejected from our world. So we celebrate the triumph and joy of this day, if for only a few, fleeting moments. The one who rode into Jerusalem on a lowly beast has been crowned the King of Glory.

Give us strength and courage, O God, that we might follow Christ, even into the darkness of night. As the clouds of fear and despair hover over the final days of his life, let us feel the anguish within our souls, knowing that Christ suffered for us. The judgment upon Gethsemane is a judgment upon all of us.

Yet through your mercy and love, we look to the light of Easter morning. We take this journey to Jerusalem because we know that Christ is with us. We know all too well the struggles between doubt and certainty, temptation and strength, life and death. Let Christ be our guide, and bless us with his saving power.

The shouts of "hosanna" proclaim the hope in which we live. And so, we remember the palms this day, as we remember who we are. Amen

39. *(For Easter)*

O God of eternal love: We thank you for the joy of Easter morning. Fill us with your peace as it flows from the risen Christ.

We have been on a journey of faith where we have encountered the passion of our Lord. We remember the long road to Jerusalem and how fragile life is. We have experienced the solemnness of the Last Supper and the darkness of Good Friday, and the images remain of suffering and death upon the cross.

But now the light breaks in. Christ returns again in power and glory. Weakness has been turned into strength; suffering gives way to hope; and love conquers evil.

Help us to share in these promises, O God, as you have revealed them in the giving of your Son. Free us from all that is harmful, now that the bondage of sin has been broken. Give us the assurance that we can always be better people and fulfill your plan for our creation.

As we leave this place of worship today, to return to our homes, our neighborhoods, our schools, and our places of work, we will remember what we have experienced here, and call to mind the wonder and hope of this event.

New life begins at Easter. The old has passed away and the new has come. The tomb and the cross are empty. Christ is not there any more. He is above us; he is among us; he is within us; and by his power, he draws us to the very heights of all that we can be. In his name we pray, Amen

2 Corinthians 5:17

40. *(For Sunday after Easter)*

Almighty and everlasting God: We come together as a community of faith, each with our own hopes and dreams, each with our own burdens and needs, but we all come seeking the Christ. You have sent us your Son, who walked among us upon the earth, so that we may follow in his ways. Help us to be more like him, for he has shown us the highest good in our humanity.

You have taken us to the mountaintop of Easter, and the inspiration of that moment lives on in us. We are renewed in spirit, knowing that Christ has come again in power, and that he shall reign forever and ever. We come today to reaffirm our Easter faith and to rededicate our lives toward the hope which we have received.

We know that life is full of opportunity, and that you affirm us for who we are and what we seek to become. You have given your love to us in a very personal way, for Christ is not only our Savior, but also our friend. Let us feel the spiritual energy which flows out of our faith, and let it guide us in all the work that we do and in all the relationships that we hold dear.

Whatever may be our accomplishments upon the earth, we return all glory and honor unto you, O God, for you have glorified your Son in order to make us whole. May the risen Christ continue to dwell in our hearts and in every place of our world. Amen

6

1.   O Lord our God, who upholds all those who are falling, and raises up all who are bowed down: You are faithful in all your works and loving in all your deeds. You open wide your hand, and satisfy the needs we bring before you.

Let all the peoples of the earth speak of the glory of your reign, and we shall repeat their blessings. Amen

Psalm 145:10-18

2.   Gracious and Loving God: We present these offerings before you, asking that they may be a blessing unto others, and that in our giving, we may draw nearer to you.

Help us to seek the treasures of heaven, rather than the things of earth; for our source of hope and confidence is in the saving grace of our Lord Jesus Christ. Amen

3.   Almighty God, the source of all good things: There are no limits upon the blessings you have given us. We now respond with grateful hearts through the offerings we bring before you, and we pray that others will join us in our song of thanksgiving.

May these gifts be a symbol of your love for all of creation and an expression of our love for you. We pray in the spirit of Jesus. Amen

2 Corinthians 9:6-11

4.   Gracious God: Bless all those, who with a joyful heart and a generous spirit, take hold of your word, and bear the fruit of your good will.

Through these gifts which we return unto you, help us to bring healing to the sick, comfort to the lonely, justice to the oppressed, and a message of hope to all who call upon your name. Amen

Luke 8:15, Isaiah 1:17

5.   Dear God, the fountain of life and light: Freely we give of our gifts, and freely we give of ourselves. For we do not live by bread alone, but by the love of Christ, which fills our hearts and moves us to share his love with one another.

Let us be your faithful servants, working toward the good of creation and the glory of your kingdom. We ask in Jesus' name, Amen.

Matthew 4:4

6.   O God of all creation: We do not wait upon the harvest, for the harvest of your love and mercy is already here. You let us reap that for which we did not sow, and we are grateful for the many blessings from your hand.

Now we return our gifts unto you and dedicate them to your service. Through these gifts, let the light of our faith shine like the dawn, so that we too, may be a blessing unto others. We pray in Jesus' name. Amen

John 4:31-38

7.   Dear God: With all that we have, help us to be content; and in our contentment, to be grateful; and in our gratitude, to be generous; and in our generosity, to share the love of Christ with all those in need. We ask in his name, Amen.

8.   Creator God, from whose bounty we have all received: Accept our offerings as an expression of our love, and so follow them with your blessing, that they may promote peace and charity among all people, and advance your kingdom on earth as it is in heaven. Amen

9.   Almighty and merciful God: We are challenged by your Gospel, which has been revealed to us in Christ Jesus. Help us to trust in your word and respond with the offering of our gifts in a spirit of true faithfulness. For you have taught us to serve rather than be served; to give rather than receive; and to love even when we do not understand. Strengthen us for your work in the world, as we seek to follow in the way of Christ. Amen

10.   Dear God: Make us willing to forego some of our pleasures in life so that others may have the necessities of life. Let us join together with hearts and hands and voices to be the messengers of your good will in the world. Let our prayers and offerings today represent our commitment to serving you and one another, according to the example of Christ our Lord. Amen

11.   Almighty God: Your Spirit moves us to be faithful stewards of all that you have given us, as we offer our gifts in love and service for all humankind. Grant us your wisdom and power, that we may spread the gospel message with acts of healing, teaching, and proclaiming your word, through Christ our Lord. Amen

12.   O Lord our God, from whom all things come and for

whom we exist: You have shown us the true way of life through your Son, the Christ. Just as he came into the world to serve rather than be served, so may we follow in his path through the giving of our gifts, our witness, and our very selves, for the good of humankind and the glory of your name. Amen

Mark 10:41-45

13.   Almighty God: We come together as one community of faith, but we are also part of the great mix of humanity. We give thanks for your love, by which you bless the whole earth and each one of us. Help us to be faithful stewards, as we join with others, to dedicate our time, our abilities, our affections, and our resources for the work of your earthly kingdom. We pray in Jesus' name. Amen

14.   Dear Heavenly Father, the giver of every good and perfect gift: You have taught us that our lives are not made secure by what we own, but by what we believe.

Grant us the wisdom of faith, so that we may discern the true gifts of life — the depth of your mercy, the beauty of the earth, the love of family, and the fellowship of your church. Amen

15.   O God of mercy: Your Spirit is upon us to bring good
            tidings to the poor;
        to comfort those who mourn;
        to bind up hearts that are broken; and
        to set at liberty those who are oppressed.
        Help us to fulfill this ministry in Christ as we offer
            up our gifts and service in his name. Amen

Isaiah 61:1-2

16.   We come before your altar, O God, that you may know us by our gifts. Let us show kindness, and compassion, and generosity, which flow from heavenly power.

May our offerings extend unto more and more people, and create in each of us a spirit of thanksgiving that will glorify your name to the ends of the earth. Amen

2 Corinthians 9:6-11, 4:13-15

17. *Leader:* What can we return to the Lord for his goodness unto us?
People: **A thanksgiving sacrifice we will make.**
Leader: Let us give unto the Lord with great joy and gladness.
People: **We will offer our gifts and our service for the glory of God!**

Psalm 116:12-18

18. *Leader:* Brothers and sisters, let us be compassionate toward one another,
People: **As God is compassionate toward us.**
Leader: Let us give of ourselves and our gifts,
People: **And we will receive much in return.**
Leader: How good is the Lord to us!
People: **We give thanks for his saving help! Amen**

Luke 6:36-38

19. *Leader:* The Lord works wonders over all the earth.
People: **His greatness cannot be measured!**
Leader: Yet he cares for each one of us,
People: **And provides for our needs each day.**
Leader: Then let our joy be in the God of all creation.
People: **And we will give of our gifts with a joyful spirit! Amen**

20. *Leader:* My soul gives thanks to God.
    People: **With all my heart, I will praise his name.**
    Leader: We remember the Lord in all his kindnesses,
    People: **And in the love and mercy he has shown through all the ages.**
    Leader: So let us return our thanks unto God,
    People: **And forget none of his blessings. Amen**

Psalm 103:1-5

21. *Leader:* Give to the Lord, all people of his faith.
    People: **We give to the Lord for the glory of his name.**
    Leader: Bring your gifts with a thankful heart,
    People: **And we will sing with joy to the God of all the earth! Amen**

Psalm 96:7-10

22. *Leader:* Let us share in the blessings of our Lord,
    People: **Who made heaven and earth.**
    Leader: The heavens belong to the Lord,
    People: **But the earth he has given to us.**
    Leader: Then let us use these gifts for the good of creation,
    People: **And return praise unto our Creator! Amen**

Psalm 115:15-16

23. *Leader:* How majestic and glorious are the works of God,
    People: **To be pondered by all who love him.**
    Leader: Let us thank the Lord with all our hearts.
    People: **For he has created wonders, so that we may enjoy them.**
    Leader: God provides us food from the land,
    People: **And feeds our soul with compassion and love.**

Leader: Let us return our praise with the offering of our gifts;

People: **For indeed, the Lord is good, and his faithfulness endures forever!**

Psalm 111:1-6

24. *Leader:* What will it profit us to gain the whole world and lose our souls?

People: **What can we give in exchange for our lives?**

Leader: Every good and perfect gift comes from God.

People: **Then in our giving and receiving, let us seek the things that are of God, for there will our hearts be also. Amen**

Matthew 16:26

25. *Leader:* How rich are the depths of God.

People: **How deep are his widsom and knowledge.**

Leader: Who could ever fathom his ways?

People: **Who could ever repay him for his gifts?**

Leader: All things were created by him,

People: **And all things exist though him and for him.**

Leader: To God be glory and honor forever more.

People: **Amen!**

Romans 11:33-36

26. *Leader:* What shall we render unto the Lord?

People: **We will offer our gifts and songs of thanksgiving.**

Leader: The Lord has shown us his works of love,

People: **And has kept his covenant with us.**

Leader: How good is the Lord to all!

People: **Alleluia! Amen**

27. *Leader:* Let us honor the Lord through our generosity,
    People: **And with every gift, show our gladness of heart.**
    Leader: Give unto God as God has given unto you.
    People: **For God is the source of all good things. Amen**

    Sirach 35:1-12

28. *Leader:* Let us thank the Lord for his mighty deeds;
    People: **And for the wonders he has done.**
    Leader: The Lord satisfies the thirsty soul,
    People: **And fills us with the treasures of heaven.**
    Leader: Let us bring our offerings before him,
    People: **And let the voices of our praise be heard. Amen**

    Psalm 107:1-9

7

1. Now may the God of our Lord Jesus Christ, the Father of glory, give you a spirit of wisdom and understanding in all that has been revealed.

   May God enlighten your heart and soul, so that you will see the hope to which you have been called, and how infinitely great is his power in those who believe. Amen

   Ephesians 1:17-19

2. Jesus said "Peace be with you. As the Father sent me, even so, I send you."

   Let us go forth from this hour remembering that whatever we do, in word or in deed, we do in the name of our Lord Jesus Christ. Amen

   John 20:19

3. The Gospel of God has been proclaimed, so let there be rejoicing and gladness among all who seek him.

   Those who trust in God will understand his truth, and will draw near to him in love; and God's grace and mercy will be poured out upon all who believe in his name. Amen

   Psalm 40:16-17, Wisdom 3:9

4. May the Lord be generous in increasing your love for one another and for the whole human family, as much as he has loved you. May you continue to strive toward the life which we are called to live, and God will confirm your hearts in holiness. Amen

   1 Thessalonians 3:12—4:2

5.   Out of the infinite glory of God the Father almighty, let Christ dwell within your hearts through faith, and let the power of the Holy Spirit keep you rooted and grounded in love, so that you will be filled with the fullness of God, now and always. Amen

Ephesians 3:16-19

6.   Jesus said, "I am the light of the world. Whoever follows me will have the light of life."
Therefore, let us be the children of light in the way that we live and in the truth that we proclaim. Let us discover what God is asking of each one of us, and surely his love will shine upon us in all that we do. Amen

John 8:12, Ephesians 5:8-14

7.   Now unto the one God, our only God, who saves us through Jesus Christ our Lord, be glory, majesty, honor, and dominion, as it was in the beginning, to this time, and forever more. Amen

Jude 1:24-25

8.   Let this be written for generations to come: that a people yet unborn will praise the Lord. For the Lord our God will reign forever, from age to age unending. Alleluia, Amen.

Psalm 102:18, Psalm 146:10

9.   In the radiance of the Lord, make your way to the light. Be strong; let your heart take courage, all you who hope in the Lord. Amen

Baruch 4:2, Psalm 31:24

10.   Jesus said, "I have come so that you may have life, and have it to the fullest."

So let us turn our hearts toward the love of God and the grace of our Lord Jesus Christ. And may God strengthen us in all the good that we do. Amen

John 10:10

11.   Dedicate your life to the Lord, and you will belong to his kingdom and dwell secure. Have hope in him; hold firm in your faith, and take heart. Yea, hope in the Lord! Amen

Psalm 27:14

12.   Blessed be the name of the Lord, from this time forth and forever more. From the rising of the sun, to its setting, let us praise God's name and give thanks for the good he has given us. Amen

Psalm 113:2-3 (RSV)

13.   Go now in peace. Remember that God loves you. And in all that you do, serve him and one another. Amen

14.   Now unto him who loves us and has established his kingdom on earth, be glory and honor from this time forth and forever more. Amen

15.   God will make you worthy of his call, and by his power, he will fulfill all of your purposes for good, and complete all that you have been doing through faith; because in this way, the name of our Lord Jesus Christ will be glorified in you, and you in him. Amen

2 Thessalonians 1:11-12

16.	Let us be disciples of our Lord Jesus Christ. For everything that is now covered will be revealed, and everything that is hidden will be made clear.

What you hear in whispers, proclaim from the mountaintops. Declare yourself for Christ in the presence of others, and Christ will declare himself for you in the presence of God, the Father almighty. Amen

Matthew 10:24-33

17.	Jesus said, "As the Father has loved me, I have loved you. Remain in my love so that my joy may dwell within you, and your joy will be complete." Amen

John 15:9-11

18.	Now may faith, hope, and love be upon all who walk in the way of the Lord. For God is the strength of his people, and he will bless us with peace. Amen

19.	Let us go forth to be faithful and dedicated servants in the work of the Lord; for so long as we serve the Lord our God, our labor is not in vain. Amen

20.	May peace and grace be yours, as you grow in the love and knowledge of our Lord Jesus Christ.

By his power, he has given you everything you need for a life of devotion and for life itself, and he calls you to share in his goodness and glory. Amen

2 Peter 1:2-3

21.	Of this we can be sure: that the love of God will last

forever. Proclaim his truth through all the ages; and for this day, let us find our joy in him. Amen

Psalm 89:1-2, 15-16

22.   Jesus said, "Love one another as I have loved you; and through this love, you will know that you are my disciples."

And now may these words be written upon your heart, as you receive the Gospel which is proclaimed in Christ's name, for you are all partakers of his grace and glory. Amen

John 13:35

23.   Now unto the King of kings, immortal, invisible, the one only Lord our God, be honor and glory forever more. Amen

1 Timothy 1:17 (RSV)

24.   Jesus said, "Anyone who serves me must also follow me; for where I am, there will my servant be also; and whoever serves in my name will receive blessings and honor from God our Father." Amen

John 12:26

25.   May the word of God abide in your heart and soul, as you go forth to make disciples among all peoples, remembering the promise of Christ: "I am with you always, even to the end of time." Amen

Matthew 28:16-20

26.   All those in Christ have now heard the good news of
salvation. Receive it into your hearts, for you have been
confirmed in the promise of the Holy Spirit, which brings
you freedom as a people of God, and calls you to proclaim
his glory. Amen

Ephesians 1:13-14

27.   May the glory of the Lord fill your hearts and minds,
and guide you in everything that you do. For God will keep
your life, and in him you will have a home forever. Amen

Psalm 37:39-40

28.   May the God of peace fill your lives with the power
of the Holy Spirit, and keep you safe from all harm. Hold
on to what is good, and let the Spirit increase within you.
        Be joyful in your life, and in all things, give thanks
to God. For he has called you to a life of faith, and he
will not fail you. Amen

1 Thessalonians 5:16-24

29.   Let us be united in heart and mind and soul, as we give
glory to the God and Father of our Lord Jesus Christ.
        For his is an everlasting kingdom, and his truth will
endure from age to age. Amen

Romans 15:4-9, Psalm 145:13

30.   Jesus said, "If you make my word your home, then,
indeed, you will be my disciples; you will know the truth,
and the truth will make you free." Amen

John 8:31

31.   Now may the God of Power fill you with his Holy
Spirit to complete all the good work begun in you. May
your love for one another increase more and more,
together with true knowledge and discernment, so that you
will always choose what is right, and so glorify your
heavenly Father. Amen

Philippians 1:6-11

32.   The things we have heard and understood, the things
that have been proclaimed unto us, we will tell to the next
generation: the glories of the Lord and his might.
    We will rejoice in the blessings of God, and keep his
commandments close to our hearts, and set our hope in
his love. Amen

Psalm 78:3-8

33.   May the Gospel of our Lord Jesus Christ come upon
you not only through words, but as the power of the Holy
Spirit working within you.
    Receive his truth with confidence and assurance, know-
ing that through faith, hope, and love, you will accomplish God's work in the world. Amen

1 Thessalonians 1:2-5

34.   Hear the words of the Lord: "I myself will be the
shepherd of my sheep. I will seek the lost and bring back
the stray. I will bandage up the wounded and give strength
to the weak. I will rescue them from wherever they have
been scattered and I will show them where to rest." Amen

Ezekiel 34:11-17 (RSV)

35. *Leader:* Since we live by the Spirit,
    People: Let us also follow the Spirit.
    Leader: What more does the Lord require of us?
    People: Only this: to do justice, to love kindness, and to walk humbly with our God.
    Leader: Amen

Galatians 5:25, Micah 6:8 (RSV)

36. *Leader:* Choose this day whom you will serve.
    People: As for us, we will serve the Lord.
    Leader: God takes delight in the people who serve him,
    People: And he will fulfill his purposes in us.
    Leader: Let us proclaim his word unto the ends of the earth,
    People: And his word shall stand forever. Amen

Joshua 24:15, 18, Psalm 49:4-9

37. *Leader:* We have received peace, grace, and mercy from our Savior, Jesus Christ. And now, what does he ask of us?
    People: To love the Lord our God with all our heart, with all our soul, and with all our strength.
    Leader: Then what more shall we say?
    People: Here am I, Lord, that I should do your will.
    Leader: Amen

Deuteronomy 10:12-22

38. *(For Christmas)*

In the quietness of this hour,
In the assurance of God's abiding love,
In the joy of a child born in Bethlehem,

In the hope that our dreams find fulfillment in him,
May all the paths you walk in be lighted with peace. Amen

39. *(For Christmas)*

Now may the peace of Christmas dwell within your
hearts, and in your homes, and in every corner of the
world. Jesus is born. Alleluia, Amen.

40. *(For Epiphany)*

Jesus said, "I am the light of the world, and whoever
believes in me will not remain in darkness."
Let us journey forward as servants of the Gospel,
remembering that the Lord will be our everlasting light,
and his glory will be seen in us. Amen

John 12:46, Isaiah 60:19

41. *(For Lent)*

Jesus said, "Because I live, you will live also. One day
you will understand that I am in the Father, and you are
in me, and I in you."
"Whoever receives my commandments and keeps
them, will be the one who loves me; and whoever loves
me will be loved also by my Father." Amen

John 14:19-21

42. *(For Easter)*

Arise and shine, for your light has come, and the glory
of the Lord has risen upon you! Go out in joy and peace,

and the mountaintops before you will break forth into singing, and the rivers will clap their hands.

This is the wonder for which we were made! Amen

Isaiah 60:1, 19

43. *(For Eastertide)*

You have been raised to new life in Christ. Therefore, set your heart upon the things which are of heaven, where Christ is sitting at the right hand of power from God, the Father almighty; and you too, will receive this power for doing God's work in the world and sharing in the glory of the risen Christ. Amen

Colossians 3:1-4

44. *(For Pentecost)*

May God fill you with the knowledge of his will, and with all the wisdom and understanding which his Spirit brings to you, so that you will be able to live a life worthy of the Lord, and fulfill his work in the world.

May you be strengthened by God's glorious power, and may you dwell within his kingdom of light. Amen

Colossians 1:9-12

8

Prelude

Morning Greetings and Congregational Announcements

Choral Introit

Opening Sentences

Minister: Grace and peace to you from God our Father and the Lord Jesus Christ. We have been born anew to a living hope through the resurrection of Christ, and we look forward to all the blessings which God promises us in him. So let us worship God; let us pray:

Invocation

Minister: Eternal God our Father, who is merciful to all because you can do all things: We thank you for your love which extends to every part of your creation. Surely your imperishable Spirit is in all of us.

In this service of worship, as you open the table of your blessings unto us, let us also open our hearts unto you and to the living Christ. In his name we pray. Amen

Hymn of Praise

The Call to Confession

Minister: The Lord is close to all who call upon him, to those who call upon him in spirit and in truth. Let us draw near to God through our prayers of confession.

Psalm 145:18

Prayer of Confession

People: Almighty God, our source of strength and salvation: We do not hide our guilt from you, but confess our transgressions against your holy will. Help us to understand our actions, for we do not always do the good that we intend to do, but carry out the sinful things we do not want to do.

Restore us to our true selves, so that the power of sin will not control our lives. Let your grace and peace dwell within us, and guide us in the ways that lead to life eternal. Amen

Romans 7:18-25

Words of Assurance

Minister: Hear the good news: God forgives our guilt and heals us from our sufferings. He surrounds us with love and compassion through the saving power of his Son, Jesus Christ.

Psalm 103:3-4

People: How great is the mercy of God! Amen

Anthem

Ascription of Glory *(in unison)*

Glory be to the God and Father of our Lord Jesus Christ,

who has blessed us with all the spiritual blessings of heaven. Before the world was made, God chose us to be a holy people, and to live through love by his abiding presence.

God determined that we would become his children through Jesus Christ, and fulfill his purposes in the world. We praise the glory of God's grace, which was freely given by the sacrifice of his beloved Son, whose blood was shed for us and for the forgiveness of sins. Amen

Ephesians 1:3-10

Gloria Patri

Prayer of Intercession

Leader: We remember in prayer all the people of the world who seek liberty, equality, and human dignity. We lift up the needs of the hungry, the homeless, and the disadvantaged. Let us pray to the Lord.

People: **Lord, hear our prayer.**

Leader: We pray for the work of the United Nations and for all other efforts which provide an opportunity for dialogue and a peaceful resolution to the problems of our world. Let us pray to the Lord.

People: **Lord, hear our prayer.**

Leader: We pray for our nation, our leaders, our citizens, and for all the important values which we hold dear. Let us pray to the Lord.

People: **Lord, hear our prayer.**

Leader: We pray for the church universal, which encompasses different lands, and cultures, and languages, but exists under one lordship in Jesus Christ. Let us pray to the Lord.

People: **Lord, hear our prayer.**

Leader: We pray for those within our fellowship who are absent from us today: those who are traveling, those who are ill, and those who are confined to homes and hospitals. We especially lift up in prayer . . . *(named by minister)* and all those whom we name in our hearts. Let us pray to the Lord.

People: **Lord, hear our prayer.**

Leader: For all those whom we love, for those who support us in the life and faith that we live, and for all of our brothers and sisters in Christ, we give thanks and praise. Let us pray to the Lord.

People: **Lord, hear our prayer.**

Leader: Dear God, grant us your peace, your grace, your mercy, and your love. Make us the people of your covenant, and grant us the power of your Holy Spirit that we may serve you faithfully all of our days. Amen

Prayer Response   "Agnus Dei"

The Scripture Reading

The Message

The Offering
   Prayer of Dedication

   Offertory Anthem

   Doxology

The Celebration of Holy Communion

Minister: Holy, holy, holy, is the Lord God Almighty.

People: **Who was, and is, and is to come.**

Minister: Lift up your hearts.

People: **We lift them up to the Lord.**

Minister: Let us remember the mighty acts of God.

People: **It is right that we should give him thanks and praise.**

Minister: We remember how Moses was commanded by God to lead his people across the wilderness, and they were tested by their inner spirit. They were hungry and the Lord blessed them with food which they had never seen before.

Because of this, they learned that no one lives by bread alone; but by everything that proceeds from the mouth of the Lord.

Deuteronomy 8:2-3, 14-16

People: **Blessed are those who hunger and thirst for righteousness, for they shall be satisfied.**

Matthew 5:6

Minister: Jesus said, "The true bread, the bread of God, is that which comes down from heaven and gives life to the world. I am the bread of life. Whoever comes to me will never be hungry; whoever believes in me will never thirst."

John 6:35

Choral Response   "Sanctus"

Minister: On the night that Jesus gave himself up for us, he sat at table with his disciples. And he took some bread, and when he had given thanks, he broke it, and gave it to them, saying, "Take, eat; this is my body given for you." Then he took a cup, and when he had given thanks, he gave it to them, saying, "Drink of this, all of you; this is the cup of the new covenant, poured out for you and for many for the forgiveness of sins."

The cup that we bless is a communion with the blood of Christ, and the bread that we break is a communion with the body of Christ. Though there are many of us, we break this one loaf and pour this one cup, signifying to all that we are one in Christ.

1 Corinthians 11:23-25, 10:15-18

The Sharing of the Bread and the Cup

The Lord's Prayer

Closing Hymn

Benediction

Postlude

Prelude

The Call to Worship

Leader: The people who walked in darkness have seen a
          great light.
People: It is a light that shines for all the world.
Leader: God has increased our joy; he has brought glad-
          ness to our hearts.
**People: We rejoice before him, and praise him for his
          mighty deeds.**
Leader: For to us, a child is born.
People: To us, a Son is given.
Leader: Glory, dominion, and power will be upon his
          shoulder.
**People: And his name will be called Wonderful Counselor,
          Mighty God, Everlasting Father, Prince of Peace.**

Isaiah 9:2-7

* Hymn of Praise   "O Come, All Ye Faithful"
(* indicates congregation standing)

* Invocation

* Prayer Response *(congregation singing)*

   O Come, let us adore Him; O Come, let us adore Him;
   O Come, let us adore Him, Christ, the Lord! Amen

The Lighting of the Christ Candle *(Advent wreath)*

Choir Anthem

The Messianic King   Isaiah 11:1-6

Hymn *(verse 1)*   "What Child Is This?"

The Unison Prayer

In you, O God, our souls find silence and peace. As you sought us through the Christ child, born in a manger, so let us seek your will with a simplicity and humility of heart. Keep us within the paths that you walk, so that we may love virtue, and receive with gratitude your heavenly gift in Jesus Christ, our Lord. Amen

Prayer Response *(verse 3)*   "O Little Town of Bethlehem"

Our Offering

Prayer of Dedication

Offertory Anthem

The Angel Gabriel   Luke 1:26-31
Visits Mary

Hymn *(verse 1)*   "It Came Upon a Midnight Clear"

* Responsive Reading   "The Magnificat"

Leader: My soul magnifies the Lord,
People: **And my spirit rejoices in God my Savior.**
Leader: For he has regarded the lowliness of his hand-maiden,
People: **And behold, henceforth all generations will call me blessed.**
Leader: For he who is mighty has done great things for me,
People: **And holy is his name.**
Leader: His mercy is upon those who honor him,
People: **Throughout all the generations.**
Leader: He has pulled down monarchs from their thrones,
People: **And has exalted the humble and meek.**
Leader: He has helped his servant Israel, in remembrance of his mercy,
People: **As he spoke to our fathers, to Abraham, and to his posterity forever.**

Luke 1:46-55

* The Gloria *(verse 1)* "Angels We Have Heard on High"

The Birth of Jesus   Luke 2:1-7

Hymn *(all verses)*   "Away in the Manger"

The Visit of   Luke 2:8-14
the Shepherds

Hymn *(verse 1)*   "The First Noel"

Wise Men Follow   Matthew 2:1-12
the Star

Hymn *(verse 1)*   "We Three Kings"

Words From the Pastor

A Christmas Prayer

Hymn *(verses 1 and 4)*   "Silent Night, Holy Night"

                    The Word Became   John 1:1-5, 9-14
                        Flesh

* Hymn *(all verses)*   "Joy to the World"

* Benediction

* The Response   Hallelujah Chorus

Introductory Note:

This service was designed for the congregation to be seated at tables. Each table should have a white cloth, candles, and a loaf of bread, and there should be a bulletin and small communion cup at each place. At the time that Communion is celebrated, the minister should go to each table, break the bread, and pass it around for everyone to take a piece, and then lift a chalice to signify that everyone should drink from their individual communion cups.

Another nice feature is to have extra loaves of bread on hand so that each individual or family can take home a loaf at the conclusion of the service.

This order of worship includes twelve Bible readings which can be assigned to members of the congregation (this also increases the attendance at the service!), and another passage from Matthew 26:26-29, containing the words of institution, which should be read by the minister.

Prelude

Choral Introit

Scripture Sentences

Jesus said, "Now is the Son of man glorified, and in him, God is glorified. My people, I will not be with you much longer. You will look for me, but where I am going, you cannot come."

John 13:31-33

Call to Worship

Leader: Tonight we recall the life and ministry of Jesus, who is the Christ.

People: **This is a night of remembrance of our Lord.**

Leader: Tonight we gather at table to share in his Last
Supper.
People: This is a night of communion with our Lord.
Leader: Tonight we find our own place in the Gospel
story.
People: This is a night of commitment to our Lord.
Leader: Come to us, Lord Jesus, in your peace,
People: That we may rejoice in your presence.

Prayer of Invocation

Most Holy God: As we come together in worship, we ask
that you keep us strong in our faith. Help us to overcome our
fears and self-doubts, so that we will be loyal to Christ, even
through the darkest hours. With courage, let us face the harsh
reality of the cross, knowing that this is our path to the resurrection hope. Guide us in the journey we will take with Christ,
for this is the journey he took for us. Amen

Prayer of Confession

Leader: Remember that at one time we were separated
from God and were strangers to his covenant. But
now we are brought near to God through the
blood of Christ, so let us offer our prayers of confession:

People: O God of love and mercy: We come before you
with a humble and contrite heart, knowing the
depth of sacrifice which Christ made for us. We

acknowledge that his sacrifice was necessary because of our sin and disobedience. Help us
through faith to accept your forgiveness. Though
you remind us of our wrongdoings, you do not
bring condemnation upon us. We ask that by
your grace in Christ Jesus, you make us worthy
to come before his table, and share in the new
covenant which he brings to us and to many. We
pray in his name. Amen

(All pray in silence)

Words of Assurance

> *Leader:* The proof of God's love is this: That while we
> were yet sinners, and unable to save ourselves,
> Christ died for us.
> *People:* **Amen**

Romans 5:6-8

Hymn   "The Lord's My Shepherd, I'll Not Want"

                      The Prophecy   Isaiah 52:13—
                                          53:6, 10-11

Solo   "What Child Is This?"

                      The Time is   Mark 1:9-15
                      Fulfilled

                      The Call of   Luke 6:12-16
                      the Twelve

The Beatitudes   Matthew 5:1-12

Leader: Seeing the crowds, he went up on the mountain, and when he sat down, his disciples came to him. And he opened his mouth and taught them, saying, "Blessed are the poor in spirit,

People: **For theirs is the Kingdom of Heaven.**

Leader: Blessed are those who mourn,

People: **For they shall be comforted.**

Leader: Blessed are the meek,

People: **For they shall inherit the earth.**

Leader: Blessed are those who hunger and thirst for righteousness,

People: **For they shall be satisfied.**

Leader: Blessed are the merciful,

People: **For they shall obtain mercy.**

Leader: Blessed are the pure in heart,

People: **For they shall see God.**

Leader: Blessed are the peacemakers,

People: **For they shall be called sons of God.**

Leader: Blessed are those who are persecuted for righteousness' sake,

People: **For theirs is the Kingdom of Heaven.**

Leader: Blessed are you when men revile you and persecute you, and utter all kinds of evil against you falsely on my account. Rejoice and be glad, for your reward is great in heaven, for so men persecuted the prophets who were before you."

Hymn   "Lord, Speak to Me"

The Fishes and   Matthew 14:15-21
Loaves

Who Do Men Say   Mark 8:27-33
That I Am

Hymn   "Ask Ye What Great Thing I Know"

The Entry into   Mark 11:1-10
Jerusalem

The Last Supper   Matthew 26:17-25

The Bread and   Matthew 26:26-29
the Cup

The Sharing of Our Lord's Supper

The Way to   Matthew 26:30-32
Gethsemane

The Lord's Prayer

God So Loved   John 3:16-17, 19-21
the World

Hymn   "O Master, Let Me Walk with Thee"

Benediction

Jesus said, "The light is with you for a little longer. Walk while you have the light, lest the darkness overtake you. For those who walk in darkness do not know where they go. But while you have the light, believe in it, that you may become the children of light." Amen

John 12:35-36 (RSV)

Postlude

Prelude

Scripture Sentences

Jesus said, "As long as the day lasts, I must carry out the work of the one who sent me; the night will soon be here when no one can work. As long as I am in the world, I am the light of the world."

John 9:2-5

Leader: The light of the world came into our midst.
People: **But some preferred darkness to the light.**
Leader: Let us live by truth and come into the light,
People: **So that the power of God in Christ will be seen in us, too.**
Leader: For God sent his only Son into the world, not to condemn the world,
People: **But that through him, the world may be saved.**
Leader: Now the Son of Man must be lifted up,
People: **So that everyone who believes in him may not be lost, but have eternal life.**

John 3:17-21

Prayer of Confession

Leader: Let us confess our sins, knowing that the cross cannot save us unless it first judges us.

People: Almighty God, in this solemn hour, we discover who we are. The forsakenness of the cross confronts us with our own failings and weaknesses, and we experience the shame and sorrow that Christ suffered there for us. Help us to understand the part of ourselves which causes Christ to be rejected from this world, and grant us your mercy so that we may receive him into our hearts and be renewed by his love. We ask in his name. Amen.

Leader: Hear these words of hope: The righteousness of God is revealed to us through our faith in Christ Jesus. For God appointed his only son to sacrifice his life for us and make us whole again.

People: Thanks be to God. Amen

Hymn   "How Can a Sinner Know?"

Jesus in   Matthew 26:36-46
Gethsemane

Jesus Taken Captive   Mark 14:43-50

Jesus before   Matthew 26:57-66
Caiaphas

Peter's Denial   Matthew 26:69-75

Hymn   "My Faith Looks Up to Thee"

The Blood Money   Matthew 27:1-10

Jesus before   Matthew 27:11-14
Pilate

                The Sentence of Death   Mark 15:6-15

                    The Scorn of   Mark 15:16-20
                    the Soldiers

Hymn   "O Sacred Head Now Wounded"

                    The Crucifixion   Mark 15:22-32

                    Death on the Cross   Mark 15:33-39

Silent Prayer

The Lord's Prayer

Hymn   "Were You There?"

Responsive Reading   Psalm 27

   Leader: The Lord is my light and my salvation; whom
            shall I fear?
   People: **The Lord is the stronghold of my life; of whom
            shall I be afraid?**
   Leader: Though a host encamp against me, my heart shall
            not fear;
   People: **Though war arise against me, yet I will be con-
            fident.**
   Leader: One thing I have asked of the Lord, that I will
            seek after;

People: **That I may dwell in the house of the Lord all the days of my life.**

Leader: For he will hide me in his shelter in the day of trouble;

People: **He will set me high upon a rock.**

Leader: Hear, O Lord, when I cry aloud; be gracious to me and answer me.

People: **Thy face, Lord, do I seek. Hide not Thy face from me.**

Leader: I believe that I shall see the goodness of the Lord in the land of the living.

People: **Wait for the Lord; be strong, and let your heart take courage; yea, wait for the Lord!**

Gloria Patri

Benediction

Jesus said, "Peace I leave with you; my peace I give to you; not as the world gives do I give to you. Let not hearts be troubled, neither let them be afraid."

John 14:27

Postlude

9

1. *For the Local Church*

O God who dwells in all times and places: As we gather here today, we are reminded of the length and breadth of your church universal. Yet even in the vastness of your kingdom, we know that you have prepared a place for us and that you call us to serve your purposes in the world.

You have called us to be a worshiping community through the joyful expression of our faith. We thank you for the witness of our worship leaders, for the inspiration of our choir, and for all those who come together in a spirit of prayer and thanksgiving.

You call us to be in mission and to serve others according to the example of Christ. Broaden our vision to see beyond the limits of our own ideas and allegiances, and make us more sensitive to the needs of others so that we will be a genuine source of help.

We are called to evangelism, as we pray that the power of Christ will be felt among all those who are searching in their faith. Let us be generous in the offering of our love, our friendship, and our care, so that Christ may be proclaimed through us.

We are called to an educational ministry, to serve the needs of our children and youth, as they seek to know your word and live by it. We ask your blessings upon our teachers and church school leaders, that by the commitment of their faith and the enthusiasm of their spirit, our young will grow in the love and knowledge of our Lord.

We are called to a ministry of stewardship, as we offer our time, our talent, and our resources to the work of your kingdom upon the earth. Let us glorify your name in all that we do, and return our thanks for your many gifts unto us.

Send us into the world, O God, to be your church in Jesus Christ, and for each of us to be his disciple. Let us offer the bread of life and the living water to all who hunger and thirst for your sake. Amen

2. *For the Natural World*

Almighty God, author of love, giver of life: In the rising and setting of the sun each new day, we see the signs of your creating, renewing, power. You speak through the winds and the rain; your presence is felt through the fire and flame.

We thank you for the blessings of the earth and the life giving Spirit you have breathed into it. Remind us that we are but a part of your world and that trees and mountains will stand longer than the span of our years.

Help us to live in harmony with nature and have respect for its balance of life. We claim no power in the world that does not ultimately belong to you. Enable us to act responsibly, so that we will benefit not only our present age, but future generations as well.

We pray for the protection of all plant and animal life; for in everything you create, you have called it good. Help us to preserve the soil we till, the air we breathe, and the water we drink.

O God of all creation, we discover again and again that the heavens and the earth proclaim your glory. We praise you for your mighty works from above, and we thank you for all that dwells below. Amen

3. *For Work (to be used on the Sunday before Labor Day)*

Almighty God, by whose hand the world was formed:

We pray for all those who labor in life. Help us to work with integrity, enthusiasm, and purpose. We know that we are responsible to one another, so as we live in dependence upon each other's skills and knowledge, may we also live in a spirit of trust and gratitude.

We pray for the homemaker, who often sacrifices many personal goals in order to fulfill the needs of the family.

We pray for office workers who must give of themselves through their sense of teamwork and support of others.

We pray for workers who are on call both day and night, handling emergency situations, caring for the sick, protecting our community, and defending our nation.

We pray for those who work at great risk to their personal safety, and those whose work is very physically demanding. We ask that you keep them in your care, and give them the strength of body and soul.

We also lift up in prayer those who have retired from their labors, and now enjoy a time of rest. May they enjoy the comforts of life and feel a sense of satisfaction for their many accomplishments. We pray for the unemployed, that there may be new opportunities awaiting them; and also for the young as they train for a career, and await the fulfillment of their dreams for the future.

In all these ways, O God, we pray to you as the Lord of life, and ask that you bless each one of us in the work to which you have called us. Amen

4. *For the School (to be used on the Sunday before the beginning of a new school year)*

O God of truth and light: We pray for those who are involved in the great endeavor of education.

We pray for students, that their path to knowledge will

also bring them wisdom. Help them to fulfill the potentials within them, that they may find meaning and purpose in everything they do.

We pray for teachers and administrators, as they give of their time, their energy, and their very selves. In all the responsibilities which they carry out, fill them with insight, patience, and understanding, and help them to see the many rewards of their labors.

We pray for parents, as they give support and encouragement to their children. May their homes be a place of learning and nurture according to the lives they lead and the examples they set for their children.

We pray for the community, in the hope that all of our citizens will support the many needs of our schools. Remind us to be as outspoken in our praise as we often are in our criticisms.

Dear God, free us from the dark clouds of ignorance, and open our hearts, as you also open our minds, to a greater appreciation of our life's journey through learning. Amen

5. *For Public Elections (to be used on the Sunday before Election Day)*

Dear God: In this time of political campaigns, we are thankful for living in a nation which is committed to the freedom of speech and the equal opportunity of holding office. Help us to preserve these freedoms, and use them in broadening our vision.

As responsible citizens and followers of Christ, let us support the elective process through our prayers, our participation, and our concern. Remind us that our passions sometimes hinder us from making sound judgments. So let us listen for the voices of reason and be guided according to your word.

There are many differences of opinion among us, but Christ teaches us that the sun shines and the rain falls upon all of us alike. So as we look expectantly to election day, let us also look beyond it, when the work of reconciliation must begin.

Be with all those who are elected to serve, that they may transcend the divisions and rivalries among us. Let freedom ring not upon our selfish desires or narrow loyalties, but upon the spirit of one people, created and sustained by your abiding love.

Hear our prayer, O Lord, and grant us your peace. Amen

6. *For Thanksgiving (a pastoral prayer)*

O God of all Creation: You have cared for the earth and have filled it with your riches. Abundance flows in your steps, through the pastures and wilderness. You provide for our land, softening it with showers, bathing it in light, and blessing it with growth.

The hills sing with joy; the meadows are covered with flocks; the fields deck themselves with wheat; and together, they glorify your name!

On this occasion of our thanksgiving, we as a nation take rest from our labors to consider your many blessings. We thank you for our freedoms, and for the opportunity to contribute our skills, our attributes, and our values toward the good of society.

We thank you for the mixture of our cultures, blending us into one people under God. Help us to be a light unto other nations, and to further the cause of freedom and justice all over the world.

We remember those who are less fortunate than us. We lift up in prayer the victims of poverty and racism, and all those who suffer from forms of political and economic oppression. Let the word that goes forth from our mouths speak of your peace, and let us proclaim our hope in Christ as the Savior of all humankind.

We pray that you will bless all those who gather here, as we have come to experience your presence among us. Give us your guidance, O God, and empower us for your work. For we claim nothing for ourselves, but return all honor and glory unto you, and offer our thanks and praise. Amen

Psalm 65:10-14

7. *For the New Year (a pastoral prayer)*

O God of all the ages: Life surrounds us with wonder and mystery. From the depths of the oceans to the heights of the mountaintops, we are aware of your power over all the earth. You alone have created and have called it good.

Help us to accept the ebb and flow of our existence. For there is a time to love and a time to be alone; a time to succeed and a time to fail; a time to change and a time to hold fast to our convictions; there is a time for intensity and a time for relaxation; a time for joy and a time for sorrow. You have put eternity into our minds, O God, and you have made everything meaningful in its own time.

We thank you for the memories of our past and for all the people who have touched our lives in significant ways. We are especially indebted to those who have nurtured us in our faith and have affirmed us for the persons that we are. May we, in turn, be a light unto others as we share the love of Christ within us.

We thank you for the opportunities before us. We ask that you give us a renewed sense of vigor as we go about our daily tasks, fulfill our responsibilities, and involve ourselves in the great adventure of living. Help us grow into your likeness, for you have made us in your image; and let us see your goodness in others, as we also see it in ourselves.

Dear God, give us hope for all of our tomorrows. Lead us toward the destiny we have in you, for you are the source of our strength and salvation. Your love has been our link from one generation to another, and together we will glorify your name to the ends of the earth. Amen

Ecclesiastes 3:1-11 (RSV)

8. *Mother's Day (a pastoral prayer)*

Creator God, who gives us life and breath: We thank you for the special gift of motherhood by which you ordained our birth. For all the tears that have been shed, for all the tenderness which has been given in our times of need, and for the pure, inexhaustible love which we have received through the deep communion of family, we give you our thanks and praise.

As we lift up our memories in prayer and feel the warmth and affection of this day, we name in our hearts all those whom we love . . . (allow a period of silence.)

Let us affirm the special bonds of family in the ways that we express our love to one another and live together in covenant. We are thankful for the vitality of our relationships which bring fulfillment to our lives.

Keep us from turning ourselves inward and loving only those who love us. Rather, turn our hearts toward the hurts and needs which are felt throughout the whole family of humankind. Fill us with the same compassion and concern that has been shown unto us.

We pray for those who may feel an emptiness inside of them today for whatever reason, and we ask that you fill them with your hope. We pray for the ill and the infirm, that they may have the strength of spirit to overcome their limitations. Help us to preserve everything that is good, O God, and empower us to make goodness touch every life. We praise you for the promise of your word and the wonder of your creation. Amen.

9. *Father's Day (a pastoral prayer)*

Almighty God, author of eternal love: We give thanks for your plan of creation by which you provide us with the close bonds of family. Through these relationships of love, we find a sense of our identity and a source of strength in our every need.

On this special day of recognition, we thank you for our fathers. We could never know all the sacrifices that have been made on our behalf and all the struggles which have been borne out of love. But we rejoice for having received this love, and we are humbled to know that we can never return all that has been given unto us.

In all of our family relationships, from one generation to another, we lift up the memories of those who have gone before us and we are indeed grateful. We have profited from their example, and we have grown by their care and understanding. Through them, we find our sense of belonging not only in this world, but in the world to come.

Dear God, may our love be the foundation upon which we build up every form of human community, and let us give our support to the many forms of family life. We ask your blessings upon the families which consist of husband and wife, the single parent, and the stepfamily. Let your kingdom be built upon all of our relationships, that as we love, serve, and honor one another, we do so also unto you. Amen

10. *Memorial Day*

O God, our strength and defender: Just as our very lives were bought with the price of Christ's death upon the cross, so too, were the freedoms of our nation bought with a dear price. We give thanks today for those who loved country more than life.

The peaceful cemeteries with rolling hillsides and small white crosses conceal the anguish of war, the bitterness of tears, and the loneliness of death.

We do not glory in war or military might, but we lift up the values of our nation that are worth dying for. We remember the words of Christ, that "whoever loses one's life for my sake will find it." Let those words come upon us today as a vital truth.

As we honor the dead, we pray also for the living, that we may carry on the hopes and dreams of those who went before us. Let us love life and liberty; let us seek the well-being of our nation; and let us be concerned for the sufferings of other peoples in other lands. As we strive toward these ends, we pray that no one in battle for our nation will ever die in vain.

We ask in the Spirit of Jesus, Amen.

11. *Independence Day: A Prayer for the Nation*

Eternal God: As we gather together in worship, we are grateful for having the freedom to do so. Today we give thanks for the birth of our nation and for all of the freedoms and opportunities which we enjoy.

You have blessed our land with abundant resources that not only sustain life, but which also give beauty to our mountains and forests, and our coastlands and plains.

We are, as one people, a colorful variety of many peoples. We thank you for the gifts and graces which each culture has brought to our shores. Help us to live together and love one another, according to our common purposes.

Dear God, guide us along our earthly ways, that as a nation, we may be a source of help to those in need, a voice of conscience against the forces of oppression, and a light of hope to all who seek your mercy, justice, and goodwill.

We pray in the Spirit of Christ, Amen.